GLOOMY
AMAZING

GLOOMY AMAZING

The practical guidebook

By Ben Wheele

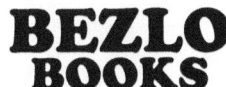

Published by Bezlo Books

BEZLO

ISBN 978-1-4116-9629-7

To Henry

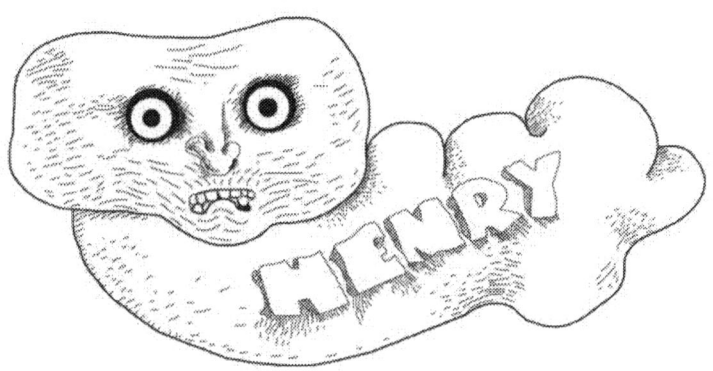

Introduction

The present volume is intended as a 'pre-career' monograph. Certainly it is being written at a point in time of which all my dealings are of reasonably low value, and this has filtered its way through into giving my Ezlo currency a very poor exchange rate. But this should not be looked upon as misfortunate - indeed the opposite! There are now a wealth of possibilities opening before my very eyes!

You should not read this book from start to finish (to be honest, actually I think you should probably just 'not read this book' but you are reading now - stubborn, I like it!) but instead read different parts for a joke yeah order yoll. Sometimes it's get, or two to find.

Many would often consider this to be ultimately a failure before it has even begun, but then how would it have materialized if most beebeen given thathat opinion of the whole thing so as not to even write it at all.

" from forth the text emerges deep problems
of which only the the most shallow can
ever begin to solve"

- Mixing Woods Post

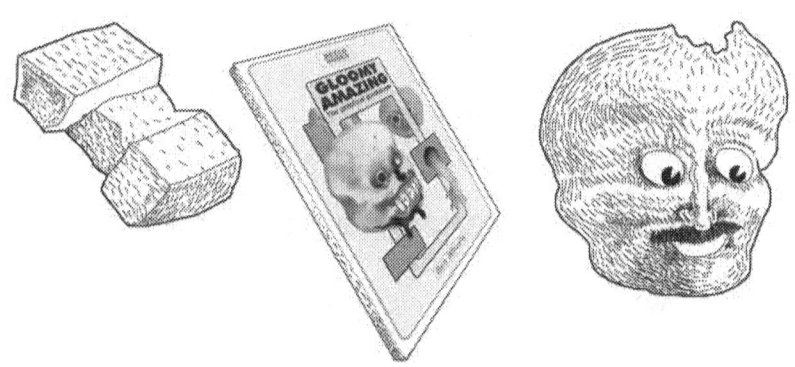

Contents

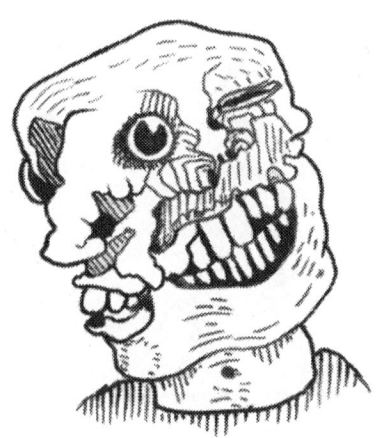
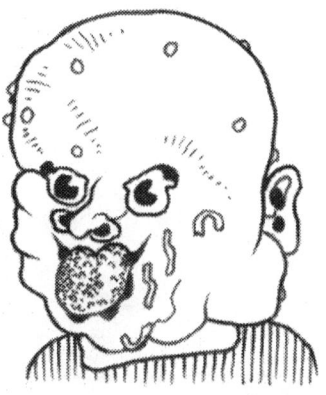

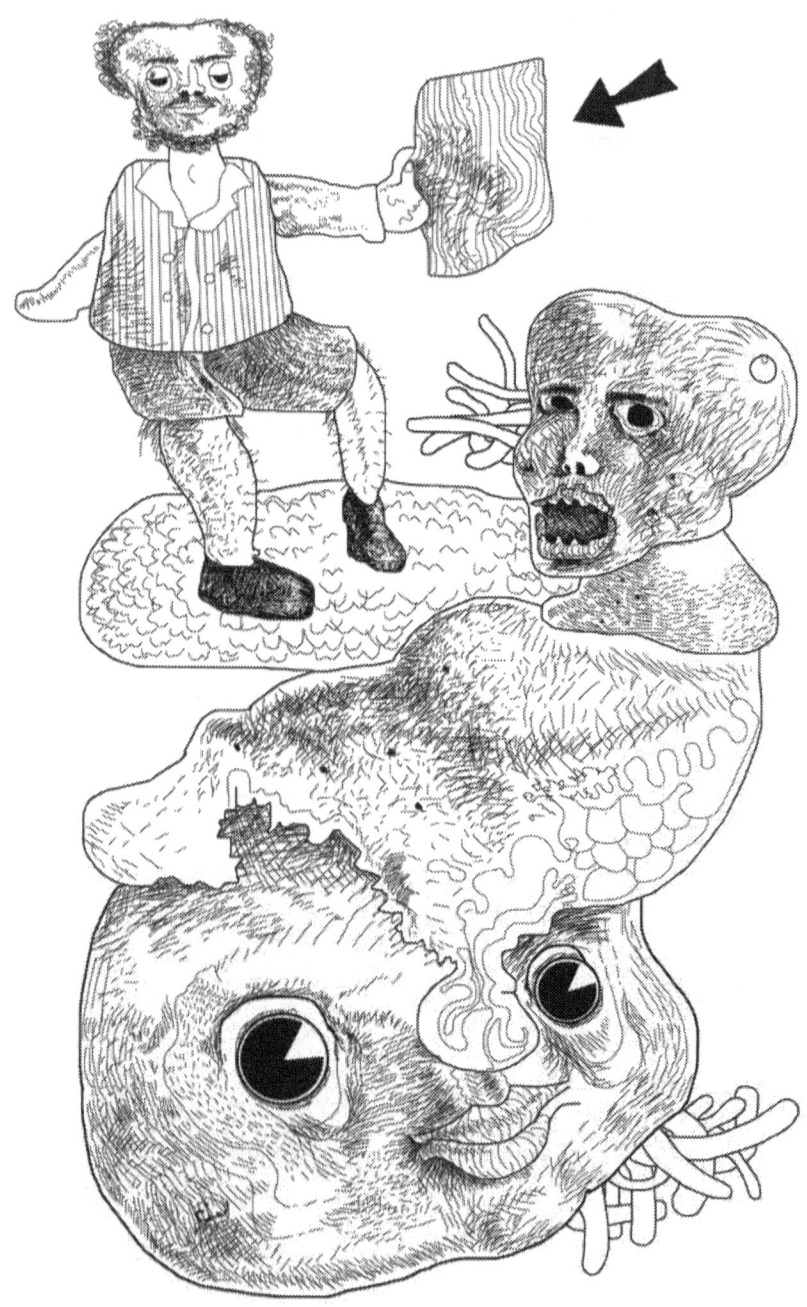

You wouldn't lie, or would you?

You stare up at his sullen eyes, wondering what he might be thinking - wondering if 'his sort' even think at all, or if they do, then how does their thought process differ from your own. Perhaps he is feeding off your current angst. Yes he must be, for as you look closer into his eyes, you sense the distinct presence of pleasure written all over his face. Check again... yeah he's definitely enjoying this. Check again... you are bored of looking now. Time to look at something else in the room.

A lampshade sits in the far-right corner. Lamp is a funny word isn't it? You agree, but argue that it is not as funny as 'banana'. You then make the point that, while 'banana' is *technically* a very funny word - hilarious even, it has, in the past been used so much in the context of 'funny words' that it has now become a lot less funny. If people had never used it as a funny word, though, it would still be really funny.

That man still looks at you. Perhaps he finds *you* funny - funny in the same way that people once found the word 'banana' funny? Again you agree, that would certainly explain the look of pleasure on his face.

Check - things are changing - he is now holding something. Check - you can now move and are not refined to this seat. As you stand up and get poised to leave, it has to be said, the man looks a little disappointed. Nevermind, for every one modicum of pleasure he gained, you lost two to angst.

Exiting the room you feel a slight chill. Obviously the man was dead wasn't he? We hadn't thought of that had we?
We? - This is uncomfortable. The use of 'we' is now banned. The pretend reason for its banning is: - 'we' is in-fact *the* funniest word ever conceived, yet it cannot be appreciated because of this very fact. To hear it in the correct humorous context would be incredibly rare. Yeah that was a rubbish reason for banning, that's why it was pretend.

You ponder on why the word [insert banned word] is banned, but not for too long - you have work to do! Two things cross your mind; the first is 'that's not fair' said by an angry American girl. The second thing is the question, 'what was the man holding?'.

You feel highly anxious about returning to the room to see, if only because he might after-all be dead, and then where would that leave us?

Us? - This word is also going to now be banned. You are naughty! You want a reason for its banning, so another pretend reason is given: - because the man was holding a plastic which is so wood-like that even people who have fathers that are carpenters, and therefore see a lot of wood, would not be able to distinguish this plastic from wood. Even if they were judged by an immortal to choose in a challenge, which one is the real wood, and if they chose incorrectly they would die, they would still maybe probably perhaps choose the plastic and maybe probably perhaps die.

Strangely, you are satisfied with that reason - not because of its accuracy, but because it was quite a good story. Wait... no it wasn't satisfying at all. There's not much that you can do about that now though, since you have forgotten what you were even thinking about. 'Ah yes!' you cry, as you recall that the man was inside the room and might or might not be dead, and that if he was dead [insert first banned word] would have nowhere to go. Nevermind, really really nevermind.

Outside it is very peaceful, it is almost easy to forget that you have a job to be doing right now. You pick up your shovel and tap it on the ground. It is cement - much too hard to take advantage of the shovel. Upon looking around you can see three main places of which the shovel may be used. Number one - a small patch of grass in the centre of the village square, in the centre of this central patch is a fountain. You could not dig the fountain, but you could dig the grass. Number two - wooden struts are holding up a marquee to the south. You could use the shovel to break the struts.

The third doesn't require any consideration for it is so appealing that you have already made you way toward it - a small boy who is sucking his thumb. No, you couldn't dig the boy. He notices you approaching and, embarrassed, discontinues to suck his thumb. The small boy is a yellow Labrador and is wearing a red cap. He really looks up to you. You mean the world to that little Tarzan. Poor little Tarzan!

How many 'poo jokes' does it take to change a lightbulb?

1. It's not to double of what you find but also to we we, hah!, fun can be un-bought because its we we is a drink but it's not don't drink urine. piss is what its other than found upside-down or normal way up. 'Shaking things' experiments are usually good, except when you make use of fizzy drinks near your eyes because its reasonable to not never maim the second largest contributor to collage this world has ever seen, its raaar! dinosaush end bu. Poo.

2. Nominate your sister for a 'biggest nose in the world' contest, and she wins and you can pay off your families mortgage, but she remains cross at you because now people refer to her as 'massive nose'. So in return you tell the competition organizers that your sister was in-fact a fake because she had filled her nose with poo-poo to make it massive and that really the Iranian man who came second place should have come first place. Your sister is more annoyed now because people call her 'poo bose'. I mean 'poo nose'

3. Why does he hate me? I haven't done anything to him! Today he broke my glasses when he threw them to Paul and Paul dropped them. I think Paul hates me too but not as much as David does. When my mum sees that they're broken she's going to be really cross and ask how I broke them. I could say that it was David and Paul but then she would tell Mrs. Roberts and then David and Paul would hate me more. I'll just say that I fell over during playtime.

4. In the previous joke, replace David with 'poo' and then it's a poo joke. In this joke replace 'previous' with poo and then it's a double poo joke. Most jokes like this one are anti-climatic, simply because to tell a 'real' poo joke would now be cheesy since they have been told so often. Lamp jokes however...

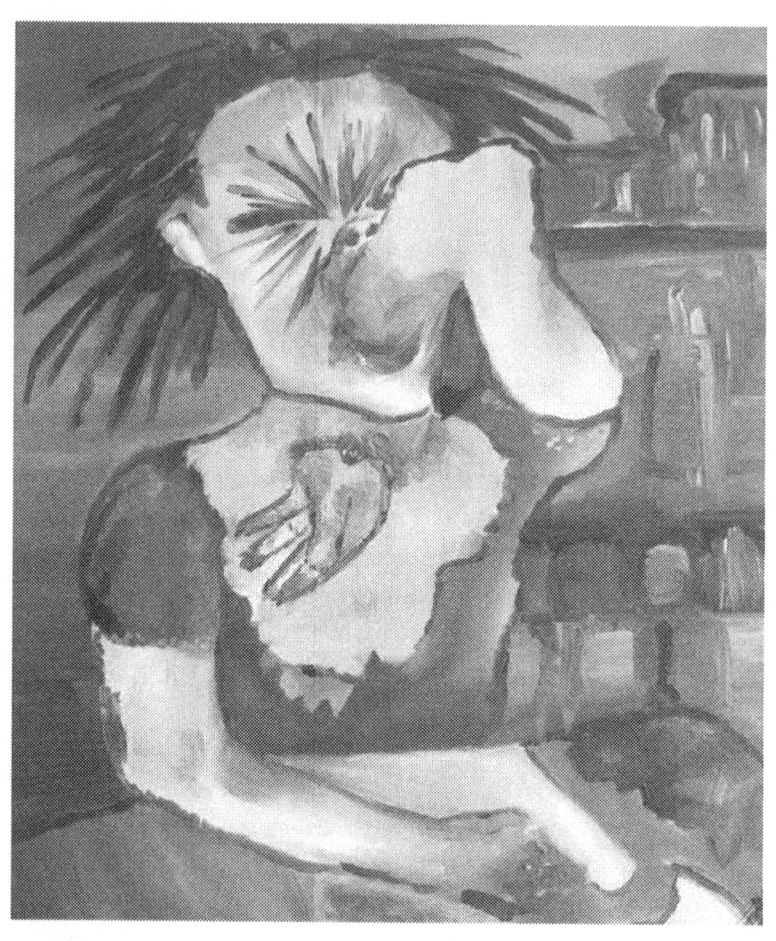

I won't live to year 2222, 2003

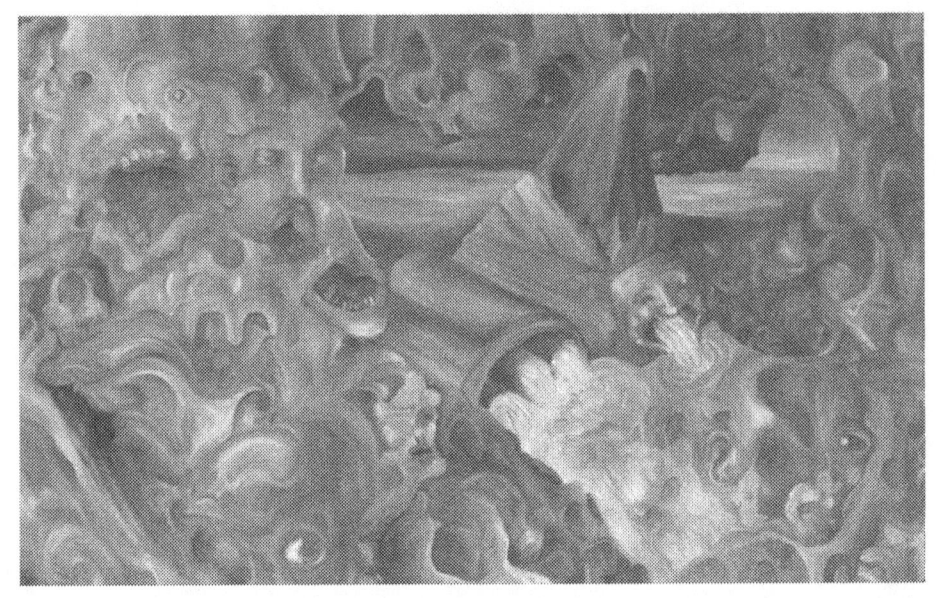

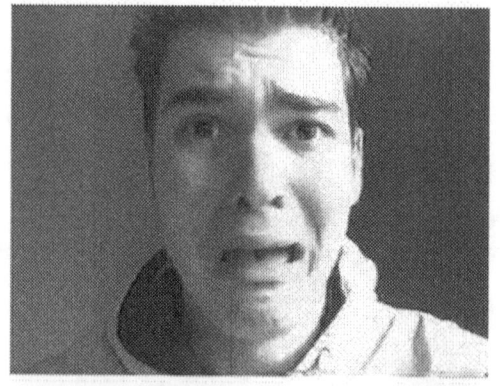

I'm not a bad man...

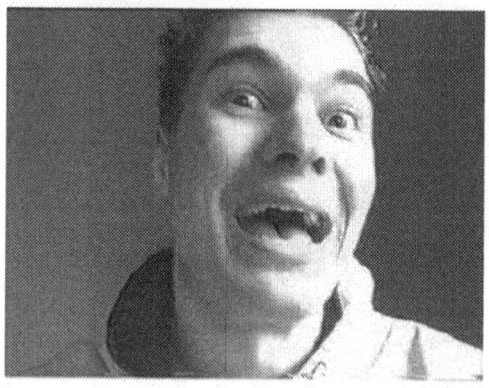

You are a bad man!

Both of these interpretations can be seen as incorrect - he is neither a man nor is he bad, or the other way round. 'He' is simply pixels on a screen. For both personas their existence is dependent on #1 him and #2 the discourse being undertaken at that moment. The value judgement that it is 'a bad thing to be bad' (displayed by the first persona) and that it is 'maybe a good thing to be bad, although I am surely not' (displayed by the second) overall suggest that the second persona *is* bad after-all.

**DVD availiable from most
good Ezlo markets priced 8.99EZ**

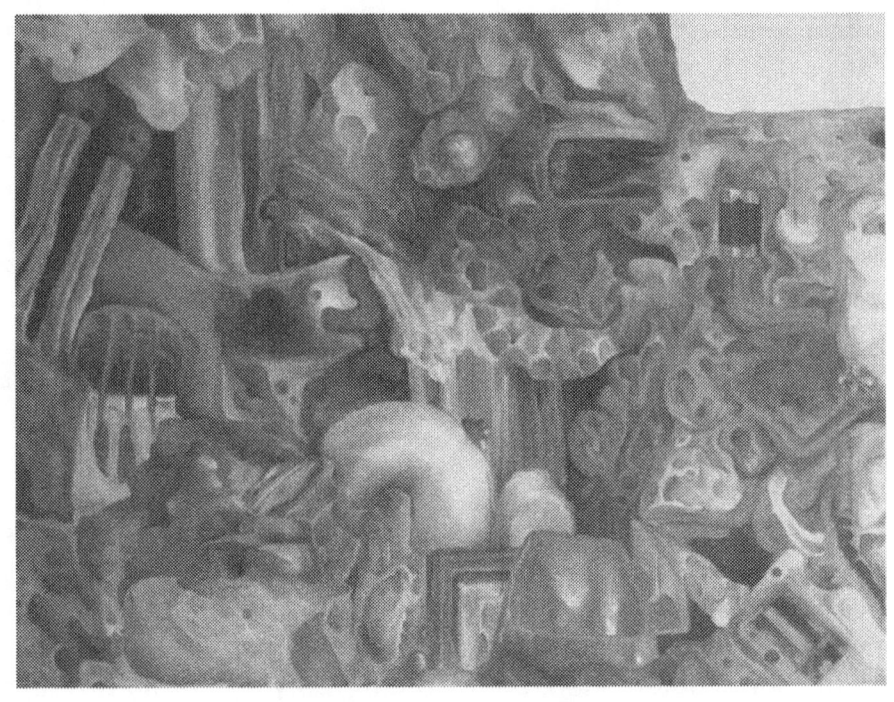

Pile, 2003

Challenge

Grey was nonetheless still scared. He knew that all those men had a great advantage over him regarding strength, and he saw that a terrifying rage had formed across each of their faces. 'Be patient,' he told himself, 'with a bad resolve I will too become angered like them and with my intellect I have a far greater advantage...yes, surely I must have...I mean it simply makes sense...'

One of the men jumped across the small wall that was farthest away, he appeared to be a leader of sorts since the others readily followed him. He wore a long patch-work-patterned suit that had been embroidered with sickly peach and pale green fabrics. Grey assumed this was a garment that had been given care and attention - albeit the care of a brutish dimwit. 'I'll definitely win this...' Grey contemplated, ' I could embroider fabric to a much higher quality than that, so that's a sign that I will definitely win this...'

The second farthest (or third closest) wall was then scaled by the group, this time with slightly less ease than the first but with all the same determined, brutal intent. Grey pulled the two ropes holding up the persuvage – they were taught. If he could only find some way to cut them – then, when the group finally descended on him, they would be crushed at the doorway, and the rest would be blocked from beyond the entrance. Upon looking around the room Grey saw nothing except some screws that were left over from the last contender participating in this challenge. 'Screws screws screws – what on earth would have left *screws*,' pondered Grey ...and then it dawned on him, the kindling tower that was outside the back entrance was heavily laden with all sorts of bolts and screws.

It first came to my attention that these savage men – the *Saual* tribe, had built this utopia of barbarianism about two months ago. As most men would be – I was at first anxious about meeting them since there was no way of foreseeing what bizarre rituals they might practice and what skewed mythologies they would uphold. But the more time I spent with them, I realized that

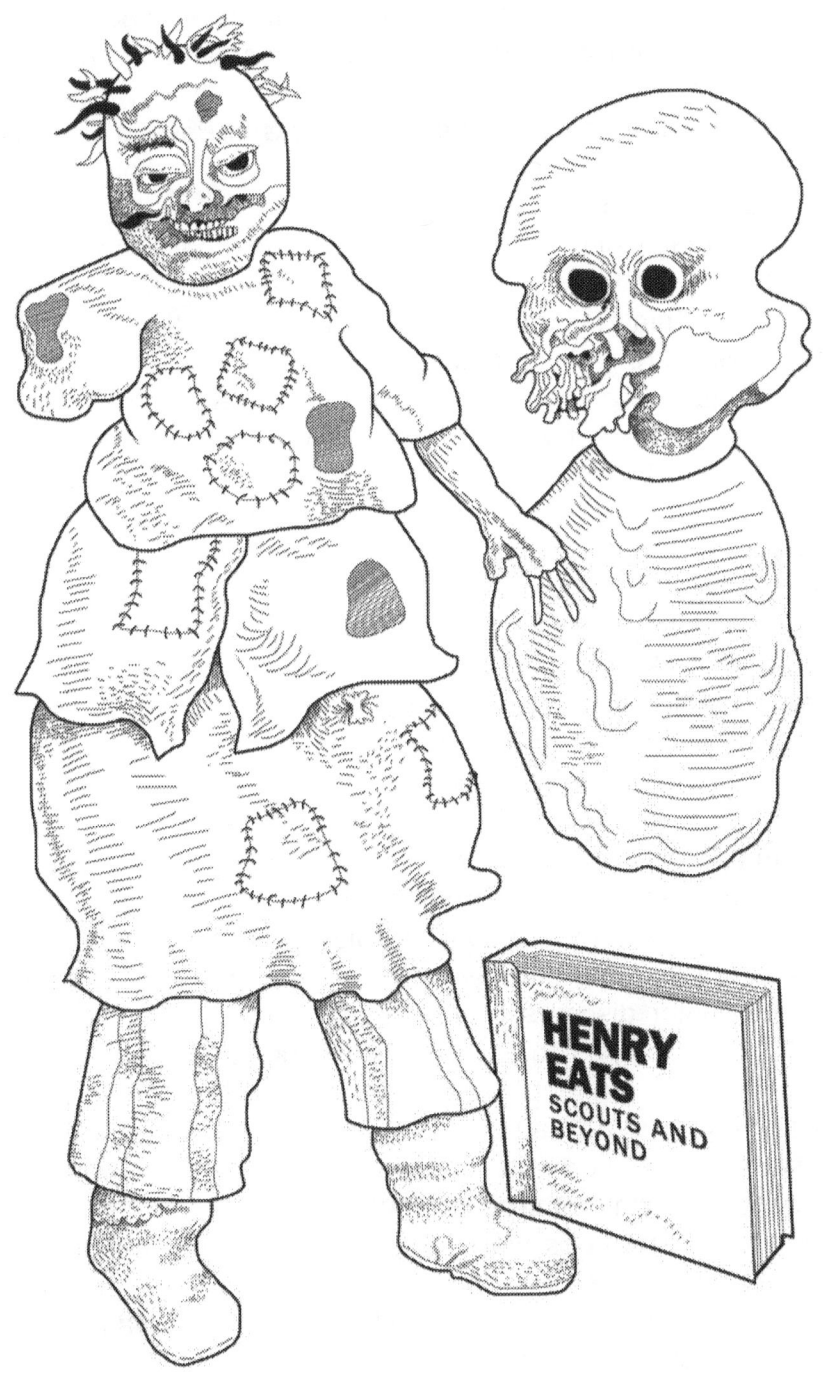

actually I was the real barbarian after all. Even when I forged a knife from wood and used it to kill some Saual with the most delicate, soft skins - I did not feel like a savage. It was only when I continued to read *'Henry Eats - Scouts and Beyond'* – a book of which I was enjoying before my visit, I felt so horridly violent and so in turn, burned it.

The Saual looked at the ashes of the book and (since the ashes were probably the darkest things they had ever seen) cried with fear. I think for the remainder of my time, the face of Lubal, the oldest, strongest and wisest of all the Saual, when he first saw the ashes, will be an image that I can never forget. Contorted with fear, his eyes bulged yet his brow wrinkled inwards and his mouth formed a curious shape, of which I can only describe as resembling a darkened hollow fist. He then choked and looked at me with this same face of terror before collapsing to the floor, dead. Other Saual then began to follow his example – it seemed that to the Saual, the sight of the mouths of other terror stricken Saual, so dark, so hollow - triggered the same reaction to that of when Lubal first saw the actual ashes.

Within about four days I could find no more living Saual on the island, an entire tribe reduced to nothing because of me. As I wondered the uglip-tinted beaches with their light sands I just couldn't figure out what to do – I didn't want to return home but staying here was so heartbreaking. The tragic crumpled bodies of the Saual were littered about the place with their distorted faces looking at me... they just seemed so real and alive – and it was in that particular discourse with myself - that odd trail of thought, which invariably led to my greatest work yet. I realised that the Saual weren't in-fact 'dead' at all! The term 'dead' was misleading to the greatest order, for while the Saual occupied a different 'state' perhaps, this did not mean they were 'dead'. After all, it is man that created death.

What opportunities were now opened! From that point on I referred to the Saual's bodies not as corpses but as little 'material prospects'. The first thing I attempted was to build a fence with these material prospects, but when I tried to hammer either their feet or arms into the ground, they broke off like pieces of bread – albeit more opportunities were born (If I recall,

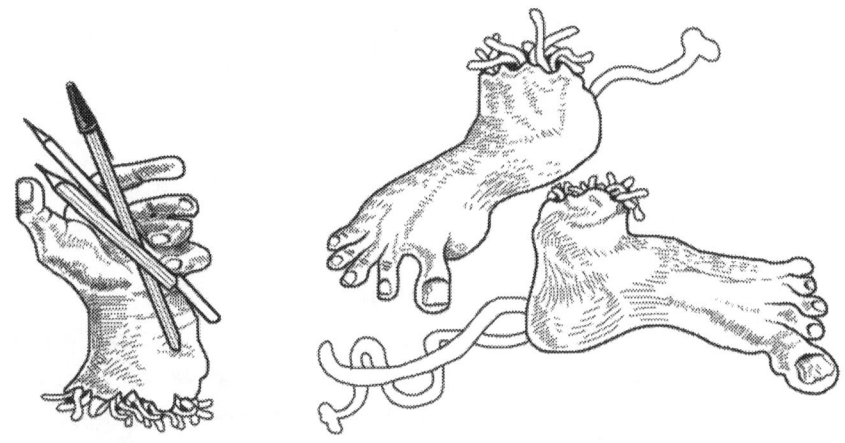

in my Studio I still have a Saual-hand pen holder and a pair of Saual-feet sculptures) but I had no fence of any merit.

It was only when I began to pile the Saual on top of each other, their stiff, yet promising material prospects really began to show some potential. I should imagine that the tower I made was easily 200 feet tall. I used their teeth to make (very convincing) bolts and screws that held up the main 'spine' of the structure and I climbed to the top using rope made from their bowels.

A further 5 months I spent on the Saual's Island before returning home. Maintaining my tower was no challenge at all since as the material prospects weathered, so did they harden, creating a tower of such rigidity that I imagined even the strongest storm would not shift it. I carved away a cavern inside the top of the tower - up until that point, there had been only negligible odours from using the material prospects, but carving away at them seemed to somehow create the most wretched stench. Luckily it dissipated within a few days. I lived up there watching the horizon for boats and such. Interestingly I never saw one boat, but always felt as though I had seen many. It was curious this feeling, troubling even at first, but it didn't stop me from enjoying my tower.

Grey had escaped his challenge with relative ease compared to the challenge that was to ensue. His daughter sat up in her bed to hear his albeit somewhat exaggerated account of what happened

'...So I was completely trapped, and the men were coming fast, I was outnumbered of course and knew that the only way to win this battle was by using my wits so I...'

'What are wits?'

'...Well...like intelligence, prowess, that sort of thing - but that really comes naturally to most men in our family, so anyway, they were approaching fast and I noticed these odd screws all about the place and saw that they had come from an even stranger tower outside the room which looked almost as though it were made from stone bodies and...'

'What? Stone bodies?' asked his curious daughter.

'Yes, like human bodies but made from this weird stone,'

'Didn't you think that was scary?'

'Not really, I didn't have time to be scared by in-animates, since there was a group of very-animates approaching me fast!'

Grey chuckled at his own joke, and his daughter smiled, not understanding.

'So back to the story, I quickly made my way out of the room and began to pull out loads of the screws at the base – you see, I knew that if I removed the base ones there was more of the tower which could potentially fall and break those ropes holding up the persuvage, but I didn't want to take all of the screws out, in-case it fell too soon, so I waited bravely by the tower until the men were...'

'The bad men?'

'Yes, the men chasing me, so I waited until they were at least within 3 meters of me before removing the last few screws and running down the side into the building. Then as soon as I entered I heard this massive rumble as the tower fell and cut the ropes crushing about four of the men and completely blocking the entrance! Before I finished the challenge and returned home I left some of the screws in the room for the next challenger to figure out what to do – that's sportsmanship you see, because even though I was against the other challengers, it was still sporting to give them a chance like one of them had given me,'

'So were the bad men the challengers?' asked a puzzled daughter.

'No they weren't,' Grey replied. At this point Grey's tone rapidly saddened.

'I think it's bedtime for you now,' Grey said, whilst giving his daughter a somewhat strained smile.

'Okay good night daddy.'

'Rest well.' Grey said, and turned out her bedside light.

Grey then walked out into the kitchen and found a suitable bludgeon, then after waiting long enough to ensure that his daughter was asleep, he completed his last, final and hardest trial of them all, the removing of the last challenger, his daughter.

Several days later Grey's wife, Lynn returned home. She already knew about him entering the competition and so the death of her daughter really wasn't a surprise. She had also been reading a book by the late Saualist, Edvard Knewvel, who had died only a year before – in his book he mentions how death is something created by man and how dead bodies are in-fact 'material prospects' of potential – so in following with these theories Lynn began (to Greys bemusement indeed!) the process of creating ornaments from their daughter, or as Grey insisted they call her, 'The toughest Challenger'.

Ear earrings, finger fiddlies, lip danglers and a liver handbag were the first few things that Lynn fashioned from her daughter's body. The truth was that Edvard Knewvel really only supported death as potential when it regarded many collective material prospects, not the one, and he even further supported the use of Saual-people for the inherent opportunities, not everyday people you might see in the shops or putting out bins for the bin men! Poor Lynn indeed!

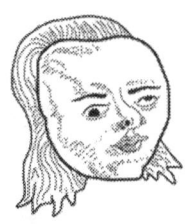

'Man, I could sure do with a better way of making Tolifu! I mean I love being an Emerald, since we have all been equal for ages now, probably 10 years and therefore everyone is an Emerald, but sometimes I wish that I could make Tolifu (our national cleaning product) a bit faster than the other Emeralds, but then again, if I could make Tolifu faster than other Emeralds, then I really would deserve to be an Emerald more than all the other Emeralds, which would ruin the whole system of 'everyone's an Emerald' sorry am I rambling on and on?'

'No no you're good, actually I'm fascinated by all of this, for in our country we only have the one Emerald, and that is not debated at all – even talking to you now would be an offence in my country, leading to prosecution. It's lucky that this is landlove!'

'Ah man yeah it's really lucky!'

'Hey have you ever done any spying work before?' Kray questioned.

'Well not really, since I've been having to make so much Tolifu recently, although having said that, I've been progressing nicely along with some undercover challenge-orientated work...'

'Ooh. Do go on!' Said a gossip-hungry Kray.

'Well I've been impersonating this man's girl-son in order to win my challenge, I've been really getting into the role too, sometimes I wonder whether myself as an Emerald really exists since my life as a girl-son is so vivid,' said the Emerald, his hands stuffing a Tolifu's slippery passage as he spoke.

'Don't say that – I can see you now and I'm talking to you through landlove, but if you didn't exist now then nor would I.'

'Kray, that's actually the best thing you've ever said to me.'

In all markets Tolifu constitutes as a bit of an anomaly. Both its relatively cheap pricing and its strength as a detergent have led to its rapid domination of not just the local cleaning markets but all cleaning markets. Studies on its properties continue to earth up more anomalies – which lead to new areas of study, and within these new areas more anomalies are bought up. This leads many to a final conclusion that when regarding Tolifu, there is no objectively accurate truth concerning its impossible properties.

One of the largest detractors of Tolifu theorizing is Klenmic Euaray, a man to whom many call 'the botch'. He wrote two books in his lifetime and both of these titles lead him into grave danger, that's not to mention the amount of difficulty he had preceding the publishing of these books.

The first is *Henry Eats – Scouts and Beyond* – the book was written at a time when there were at least 5 or 6 studies being carried out on why Tolifu was so advantageous, and each of these studies threw up new questions that invariably created another new paradigm. Euaray envisioned these as spiralling out of control and eventually becoming more important than simply having clean things and keeping them clean using detergent.

His thought was this: if on Monday there are 5 paradigms, and each of them throw up 4 anomalies by Sunday, then that's (roughly) 20 anomalies a week, now it is important to remember that some of these bizarre questions are coupled together so it is never one paradigm for one anomaly. For example the slippery nature of Tolifu packaging can include the questions 'why does ementic O9U lambaste so much faster than all other ementics?' and the question 'how can we appropriately test the slippery nature of O9U with equipment which is metaphysical?' leading to a broader question of 'is the term ementic relevant? Are ementics simply illusion?'

Of course this was all distracting to Euaray and it was all missing the point that there can be no objective truth anywhere. He printed both of his books on special papers which when set ablaze, often result in a 'pitch black' appearance - this was another controversial aspect to his writings.

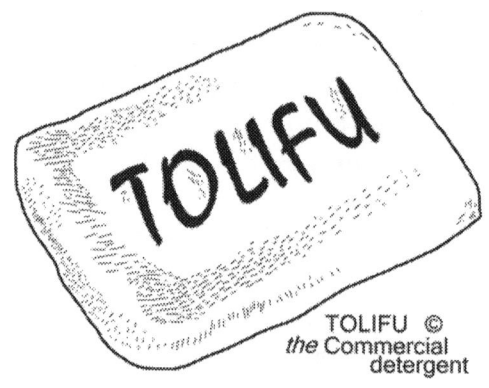

TOLIFU ©
the Commercial
detergent

The case-study in hand:
Henry Eats

Images: *Henry eats, 2005, 4:35mins, animated*
Text: *Extension, 2006*

He woke up to the sound of a woman screaming. He was lying on a bed in hospital. Unable to move his body, he managed to strain on his neck muscles, which in turn bought his head upwards for a few seconds. He could see that large belts strapped him down, and that these were not going to budge. He also saw that the room was grey with a peculiar yellow glow emanating from a window that was above his head.

This window was open, and as a result, he could feel the wind gather and subside as it swept through his hair. The scream continued to sound in short bursts, although it had changed to more of a raspy hissy gurgle. It is strange, he thought, that he did not notice the scream change from a shrill high pitched sound to its current, more grating sound. It must have changed when he was looking around the room.

He noticed that the ceiling, whilst admittedly grey, had peculiar 'moments' of colour amongst the grey. Powerful greens next to moody purples which reminded him of something thundery - perhaps when the sun is shining, yet the clouds are still dark... these thoughts briefly opened up inexplicable feelings which as fast as they materialized, dissolved back into the black sea. As soon as he tried to understand or name one of these feelings, they became watery and slipped through his fingers.

The sound of footsteps then became audible. The screaming had now ceased completely. Again he wondered how the scream changed from being such a horrible rusty noise, to not 'being' at all without his noticing. It must have been when he had tried to understand that inexplicable feeling. The steps grew louder and more confident. He imagined them as a beat, the rhythm to a strange woodland dance, with the limbs of young bodies jerking in and out religiously on time with each pounding crash of the drum. Bang and bang and thump and bang and crash and thump and boom. This was delightful. For what seemed like too many minutes to count, he enjoyed this woodland celebration of the drum. Eventually the limbs, which once jerked inwards and outwards so rigorously, now could muster no more strength. Their owners had grown old and weary of such tiresome things as dancing.

The footsteps had stopped too. What sounded like a large metal door was opened. It scraped across the ground. Metal grinding upon concrete - each surface only beautiful once married.

A figure entered the room.

'Are you the character?' It boomed.

'What do you mean?' Replied the patient.

The figure began to anger, for it was hoping for a quick 'yes or no' answer at this point. Nobody spoke. The figure had never been asked a question before. For a full five minutes it stood in silence, astonished, furious. Its little lips twisted inward with anger. Left and right, looked its tiny pokey pin-eyes. The hospital patient strapped on the bed wasn't entirely sure whether a figure was really in the room at all - had he imagined it? 'Are you the character?' - that's what it had said wasn't it?

The figure remained still. Was the figure itself now in fact the *character*? Stuck in this standing position, the figure was now perhaps now called 'Henry', not the man in the bed. Henry's eyes grew bright. In this predicament, he forgot that he was angry at all and a large smile developed across his face - almost too large, for it split muscles and tore ligaments in his face. Was he food or was he dead?

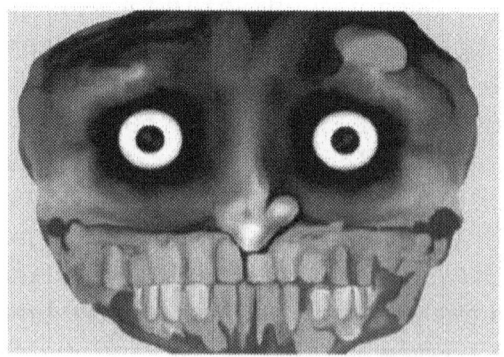

He woke up to the sound of cutlery chinking and the murmur of people talking in the distance. He was at a dinner party and had fallen asleep on a sofa in a darkened room. Someone had placed a blanket on him - a nice gesture, the sort of gesture only Henry would appreciate. He got up from the sofa and fumbled around for the light switch.

Henry then began to make his way back into the dining room where the party was continuing. 'Oh you're awake,' he imagined them saying. As he walked down the hallway outside the dining room he heard a familiar, distinctive voice. A pang of horror was released into his stomach. It couldn't be, could it? Grey Foster, the man who killed his own daughter. Listening harder now and half hidden, Henry peered through the edge of the door, ever so slightly. He snatched a quick glimpse. That was Grey all right.

There were three things about Grey that Henry feared. Firstly, he obviously killed his daughter - yes, this is disturbing of course but not the most disturbing of the three things. Most people would be sent to jail for life for such a crime, especially Grey, since for weeks after the murder he wouldn't stop raving about how proud he was to have killed her, and claimed to have completed a personal challenge by doing so. The second thing, the most disturbing thing, was that to Henry's astonishment, not one person had found Grey's murder troubling in the slightest. Quite the opposite in fact - for weeks, people praised him. 'Well done Grey,' they would say, 'you are so brave!' Henry had felt very isolated. He was *sure* that murder was wrong... wasn't it? The police didn't care at all and they had thought *Henry* to be strange for taking such offence at the crime.

The third thing wasn't so much something frightening about Grey. For a couple of months now, Henry had been seeing Lynn (Grey's wife) after work, behind Grey's back. It started when he had fixed their boiler and Lynn had been crying so he comforted her. One thing led to a scattering of other things, and each of these led to another. Eventually they were having a full-blown affair. Do you choose to enter the room?

If you enter go to page 31
If you choose to go outside, continue reading.

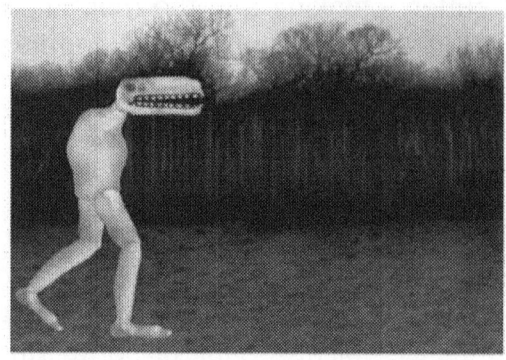

So you've chosen to go outside! Or perhaps you've noticed that this page has a picture and must be more interesting. Wise choice anyway. Henry decided that he should leave Mrs. Dawson's house and walk home.

'Mary won't mind,' he reasoned, 'I'll just tell her that I was feeling sick.'

Henry quietly backed down the hallway and exited the building through the front door. The night-time breeze filled his lungs as he walked through the darkened woodlands. A red haze tinted the sky and Henry stopped for a moment to appreciate its colour before continuing to make his way home.

Ten minutes later Henry saw something very distressing walking in the woods about 500 yards to his left. A figure with an entirely green body, bright red eyes and no arms. Its strides were almost mechanical, and with a horrible intent. Its head was peculiarly long, much like a crocodiles and, also like a crocodiles, it had teeth running along the entire length of its mouth.

'What the hell is that...' Henry thought.

Suddenly the creature stopped. It had noticed Him. Henry was struck with terror. For a couple of moments, neither of them moved, staring at each other through the woodland.

Henry then ran towards his home as fast as possible, not even checking behind him to see if the creature was following. Sitting at his kitchen table, still petrified, looking out of the window Henry was cleanly decapitated by the creature's jaw, without even noticing that it was ever behind him. But was he food or was he dead?

So, you've chosen to enter the room! Henry blundered into the room, a massive oaf, and knocked down the lampshade (lamp!). As it fell it also bought down some cutlery on the worktop, smashing against the cold granite floor and breaking into tiny pieces. Henry moved to clear these things up, but slipped over his feet and started running. He tried to stop running, but it was impossible.

'Why am I running? - This is so peculiar!' he thought, as he cascaded towards the other party members.

'You are a real mistake!' Grey snapped.

'Henry for God's sake.' Mary was livid. 'Have you gone mad?'

'I can't stop running!'

Henry continued to run at full tumble, scattering papers and thoughts across the room. The guests had now backed against the wall, watching as Henry sprinted around the room in large circles, creating all manner of havoc in the carefully furnished modern dining room.

'You're cleaning all of this up!' screamed Mary.

'It's not my fault!' Henry replied.

'Really!' Mrs. Dawson tutted, 'And it had been such a nice evening up until now,' she glared at Mary.

Mrs. Dawson's 10-year-old son Danny was secretly grinning in delight at how this boring evening had turned into such fun!

At this point, Henry thought of something actually quite marvellous. In this current unruly 'running' predicament it would be the perfect time to tell Grey about the affair, since, Henry figured, he would not be able to catch him without running too and Grey had a bad leg!

'Grey I've been sleeping with your wife.' blurted Henry offhandedly.

'What?'

'It's true, sorry, don't kill me.'

An explosion of rage erupted within Grey, his cheekbones throbbed and his mouth slowly widened forming the most curious 'smile' of anger. He imagined devouring that little piss which was running around the room. Fists clenched, Grey *was* now Henry in every way and form possible, running around the room himself. He had gobbled Grey up! Was he food or was he dead?

Questions

Q: which would you rather save, the entire species of dogs, or a classroom full of children?

For dogs: Imagine all those blind people who depend on guide dogs. Imagine them waking up in the morning to find their dog has vanished.

'Ginger...Ginger...where are you boy?'

Also think about how much drugs would be smuggled without the noses of sniffer dogs. (If you like drugs though, don't save dogs)

For children: You could train the class of children to act like dogs and replace some of the dogs, but there are *millions* of dogs and only one class of children. Human life is precious too.

A: The answer is this - dogs aren't really a proper species since they have been selectively bred by man from wolves and things. Man could eventually (over time) re-breed dogs again.

Q: Which challenge would you complete? You have a month for each challenge, after that month is up, if you have not completed any challenge, you will die.

#1: The next time a person hugs you (if nobody hugs you then you will fail the challenge and die - you are not allowed to ask people to hug you - this will also result in failure) you must make sure that their feet (including shoes and socks) do not touch the ground/floor for the remainder of the month. If they do, then you will die. The best tactic for this task - a tactic of which previous challengers have succeeded, is to 'trap' the person who hugs you and place them in a closet/basement and to use a climbing harness on them so that their feet don't touch the ground for that month. You are not allowed to tell this person about the challenge, this will result in failure.

#2: You must fill a car with as much British soil as you possibly can. The only room left in the car should be your own driving seat, the rest should be soil. This car with you driving must then be taken to America via ferryboat. To evade customs and other such problems, some challengers have painted the windows of the car to resemble what the interior of an empty car would look like, so as to not raise suspicion.

Once you are in America, you must find a group of wild beavers and mould your British soil using American water (creating mud which will dry) to resemble, perfectly, another beaver. Then you must wait until a male beaver tries to mate with your mud sculpture. When this happens you will have completed your task.

A: Both tasks are very difficult. People do not like to be trapped and hung above the ground, and customs officers do not appreciate people bringing whole cars full of soil onto ferries, so here there really is no correct answer. You would probably die either way.

Q: You have to eat one of the following, but which one is the correct one?

#1 A dead dog, which has been floating in a pond for a week.

#2 An entire street's worth of chewing gum off the pavement.

#3 A crate of cigarettes. (You must *eat* them, not smoke them)

#4 Every person of whom you are related to (including extended family) spits in a bucket and you must drink it.

#5 A poo.

A: A poo maybe? Jeeps, I really don't know on this one, it's been debated for many many centuries as a philosophical question.

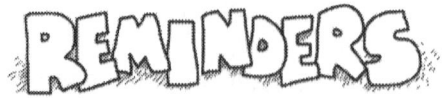

REMINDERS

Selected extracts from 'Reminders' by Ben Wheele

There is a problem, in a movie. The protagonists are formulating plans on how they might overcome it. Nobody can think of a good plan and then somebody suggests something slightly more off-the-wall. There is a silence...and then the leader of the group solemnly says down the camera:

'I think it might just be crazy enough to work...'

cut to a montage of them preparing this wacky plan

So what does this imply? well, perhaps it means that the more crazy a thing is, then the more likely it is to be successful when you are up against the odds. Take a look at this example:

An old lady down the road has been diagnosed with cancer - everybody knows her and she is a valued member of the neighbourhood. To save her from cancer, you have three options:

#1. Leave it all down to the doctors. If they can save her, then they will, but your actions alone could not help.

#2. Be really nice to her, keeping her relaxed and in good spirits, you could perhaps even try suggesting herbal therapy to her, if only for its placebo effect.

#3. Make tiny little men from tin-foil and put baked-beans inside them.

Using the previous formulae of **Crazy idea = The best idea.** The third option would be the correct one here. But why? well, nobody really knows. It's in movies - it is true.

Boyu bayd 0 mizin. It's nwo for the aldk wim nix mixing all those woods, previously happened brown one you dickstart! the brown one the brown one the brown one!!!! **** thats not brown it's deffrinatelry greay 3.

3re LOJ

I found this WICKED tactic for getting out of situatrions sdk you liek say when the woman is all walking off and upset, "I love you" in a really low voice. Then she gets like all (Bad spelling!) "what?" and you then have to say it again - "I love you"... and she sayslical 'really?' and then you have to say ' yes' (it helpsif you crya bit) So i did it6 and it really reallu worked well totally . sasdj

Sumem time sl really wonderwhat you aredoing writinga book it's stupidand yourenot doingit properly andits notart really isit, becauseit's literature. But then I rememberthat noneof that really matters matters after all because it's all just words.

Art: any definition I put now is going to be words so I've decided to put just one word, which will describe it best - ojsfjokasjdoij.

Seebecause its all just words and languagespp itt meansas that all these horribles spellings and mistakes, really do becaome 'misakes' when tehyre no diffewent, since wordss themselves are metaphors anywaytheres no 'correct' metaphors

0

        0

            0

                0

                    0

thiss now looksa really rubbish because ws it's likes ive tried to do a 'bad spelling puncturation' *thing* and the joke is that you can buy a reeaslly good kippenberger book for like £10 amd this books is gfoing to probably cost similar, and its not good at all is it? wellrd mayuhenbb ists actually bettyer ...

See? we comne to the conclusrion of ideological critique. you say that ive only said my book is better because I made it. And then I say that you only said that because your jealous and we both get nowhere atall. Ideological critique cancels itself out. Why is your company not reducing fuel emmisionsssk????? is it because you want loads of money you greedy fat-cats, because fa itsa cheaper to iuse fossil fuesl and yoiudr damagins the environment. And then Adsk Fat cats say - BWy but whysw is this group acting like it is. Maybe the ednvironmentalists are simply bitter becasue they have less money - if they had monedhy theysa damage THIS environment TOO . SEE NOW I'M entering A NEW GAME WHERE I PUT ALL ONE syllablee WORD thingies IN capital letters. SO THIS IS THE GAME correctly being played. But this would be it BEING played INCORRECTLY. Hes gotas a rewallywired achest becuas is geoes inwards wheres istsx should goes flate. So wierd in fact, that he is very very very very shyabwoyt it OH SCRIBUS ISNT CRASHING NOW>>!!

O

O

O

O

O
Sad movies aren't sad.// people are sad//

I'm not gay mrag, so I have less to be proud about? I am gay so I have less to think that I should be proud about, but really I should be?
There is an inherent idea - stemming back to the yeaaah Enlightenment that we are individuals and that we should go against authority! go against the bigwigs! be proud of who you are as an individual and stand up for it! yeah! individuals!

But yousd see - 'Individual' doesn't really exist - My name , James, what part of my body does it refer to? they are constantly chabsing changinsg chaning changing. And imnever in. The same place. At the same time. Ever again. So why do I have a name? why are we 'ones' when we might come in groups of four, or miught be a collective flow of atomsas. What everdn are atomsa? they too arre metaphors >>>>>

?

Rationality is an tradition in (or under) lots of traditions, rather than an standard of that all traditions need to conform to. (holidays)

I love life, but I haven't tried anything else, so how can I compare

Relationships are prior to all that is intelligible. Like a man who is standing, and is a relationship.

Billy Mayerl is the favourite musician ever.

A book that has gone downhill lots. Many people thought that it was probably the worst book they had ever read. For some people, English was not their first language, yet they still read the book and afterwards wondered why they bothered to learn English at all. It really is a tragic normal world. Don't get me wrong - some things were cutting-edge - like Goldsmiths College, but now it's the norm again. Order is restored. I win.

Well, perhaps now would be a good time in this book to act upon *all* unspeakable things - orgies or otherwise. For it is not my aim to encourage metamorphoses but instead I hope for us to not even think of them as metamorphoses, rather, a different form of 'game' which *understands* and accepts that it is merely a game. Wait... merely? I have just say-ed a thing of large injustice - for it is these 'games' which *become* life itself. I should be much more grateful.

I'm a naughty little benny-woo!

Lemon flavour sweets suck!
Seriously who likes them?

::::: I do

Who are you?

::::: Snelly

Snelly??

::::: no

...okay so what *is* your name?

::::: Snelly

oh, right I see, your being difficult - that's why you said that you liked lemon flavour sweets.

::::: no I didn't

you said 'I do' when I said who likes them!

::::: I wasn't talking to you - I was getting married and the time had come to say 'I do'. So I said 'I do' . Everybody in the church is looking at you, you're ruining the service.

Oh, sorry - I wasn't aware of this, how can I make it up to you?

::::: Just shut up

okay, usually I don't like being told what to do, but I suppose weddings are quite important so I'll be quiet now.

::::: Well, it's not an important wedding, it's a slap culture Salt Peanuts wedding

A what??

::::: Never mind, you wouldn't understand.

I might do, try me!

::::: *sigh* okay, well I'm listening to a song called 'Salt Peanuts' by *Dizzy Gillespie All Star Quintet*

right, and what's 'Slap culture'?

::::: Well, that's *why* I'm listening to Salt Peanuts. Well, I should say 'was' listening to, since the track has finished now. Slap culture is now about the song 'Lover Man' by *Sarah Vaughan with Dizzy Gillespie All Star Quintet*

I don't understand

::::: I said you wouldn't

If you had explained it better, then I might do!!

::::: oh you just don't quit do you? Right okay; imagine being slapped in the face...

yeah...

::::: *that's* slap culture.

really?

::::: no

I think slap culture is just a thing you've made up

::::: I think slap culture is just a thing you've made up

Are you copying me?

::::: Are you copying me?

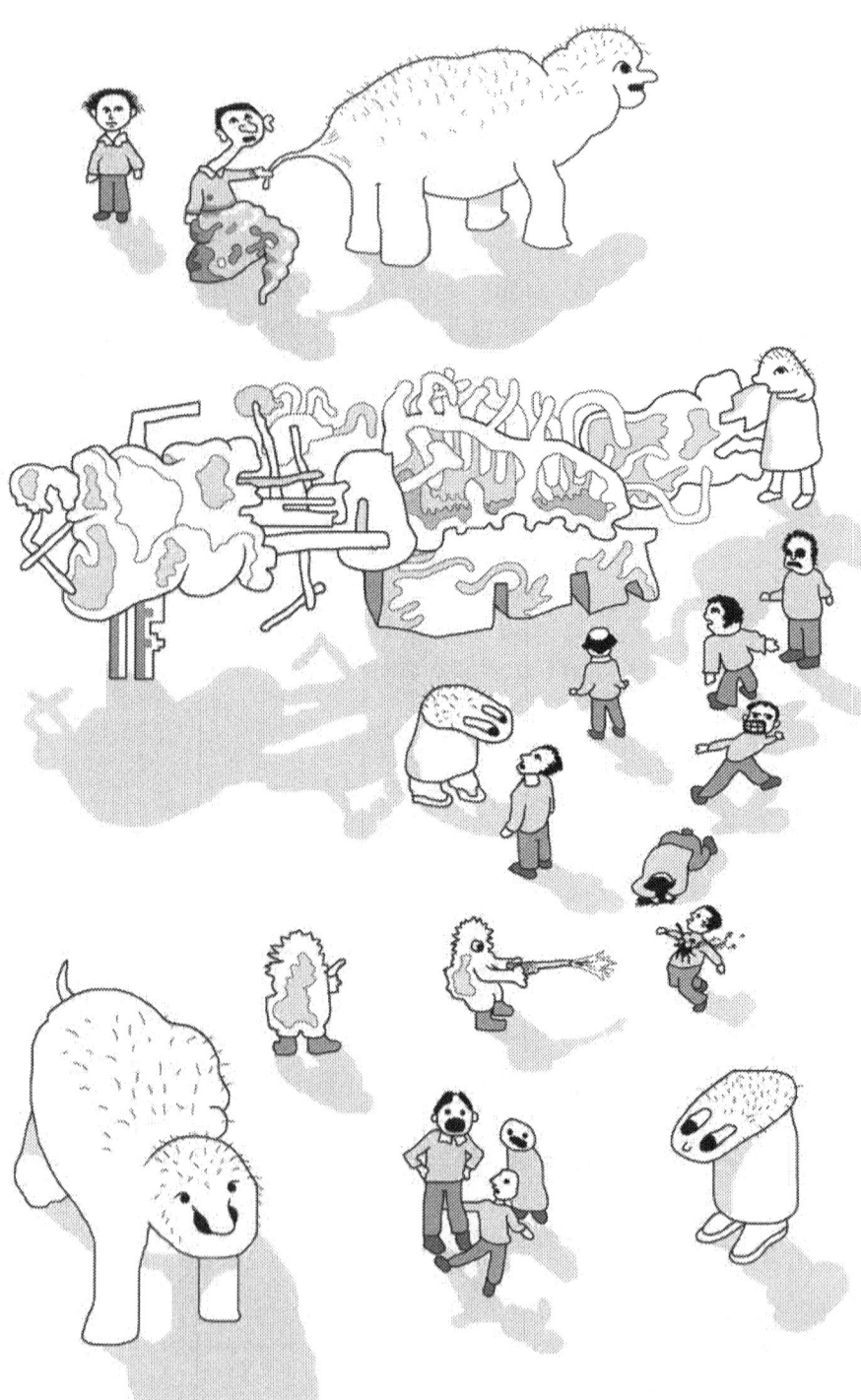

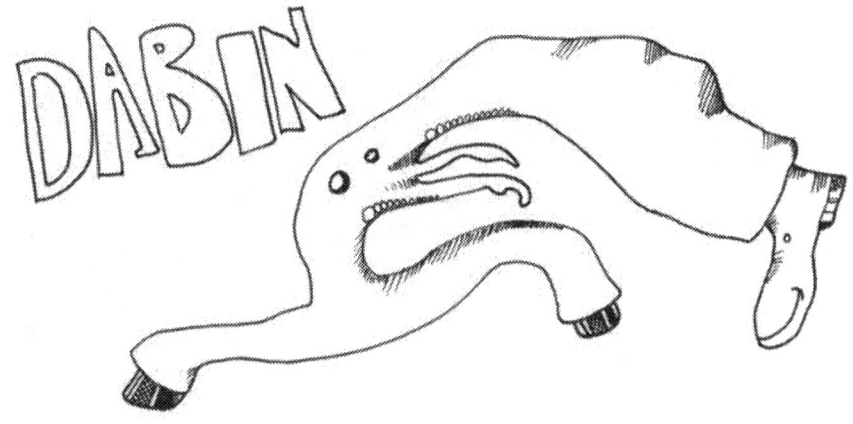

Oh it really is a wonderful creature -
and special!! Wonderful *and*
special, with a shoe for a face,
Dabin can win any race.

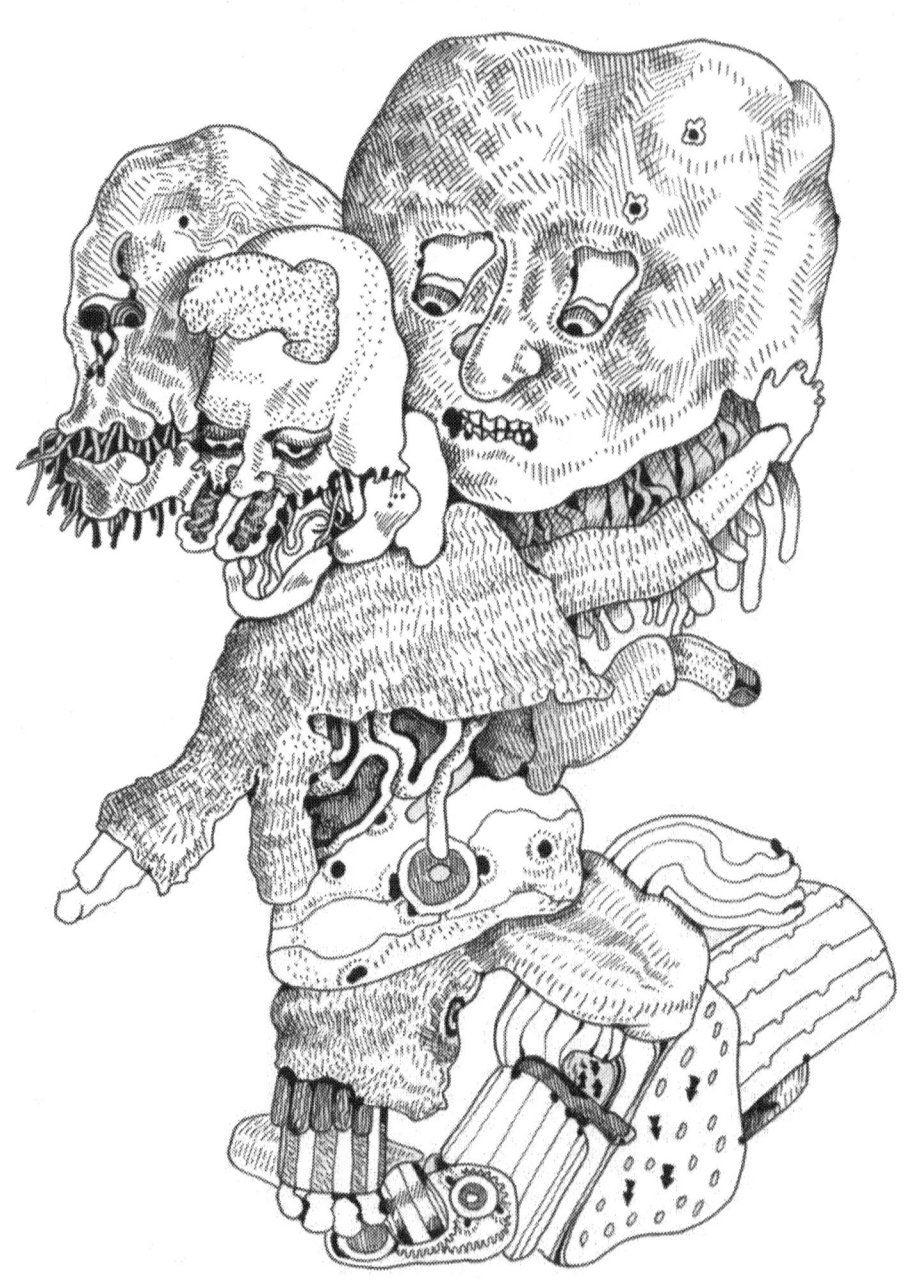

"I can't believe it! All criticisms are automatically wrong! Exclamation marks!!"
- DAMIAD HIRST

"...this is terrable terrible brillant brilliant!"
- TONY BLAIR

"If slap tourism were really bad, wouldn't that force it into being really good anyway?"
- MEZLO

"I'm not even alive anymore!"
- ANDY WARHOL

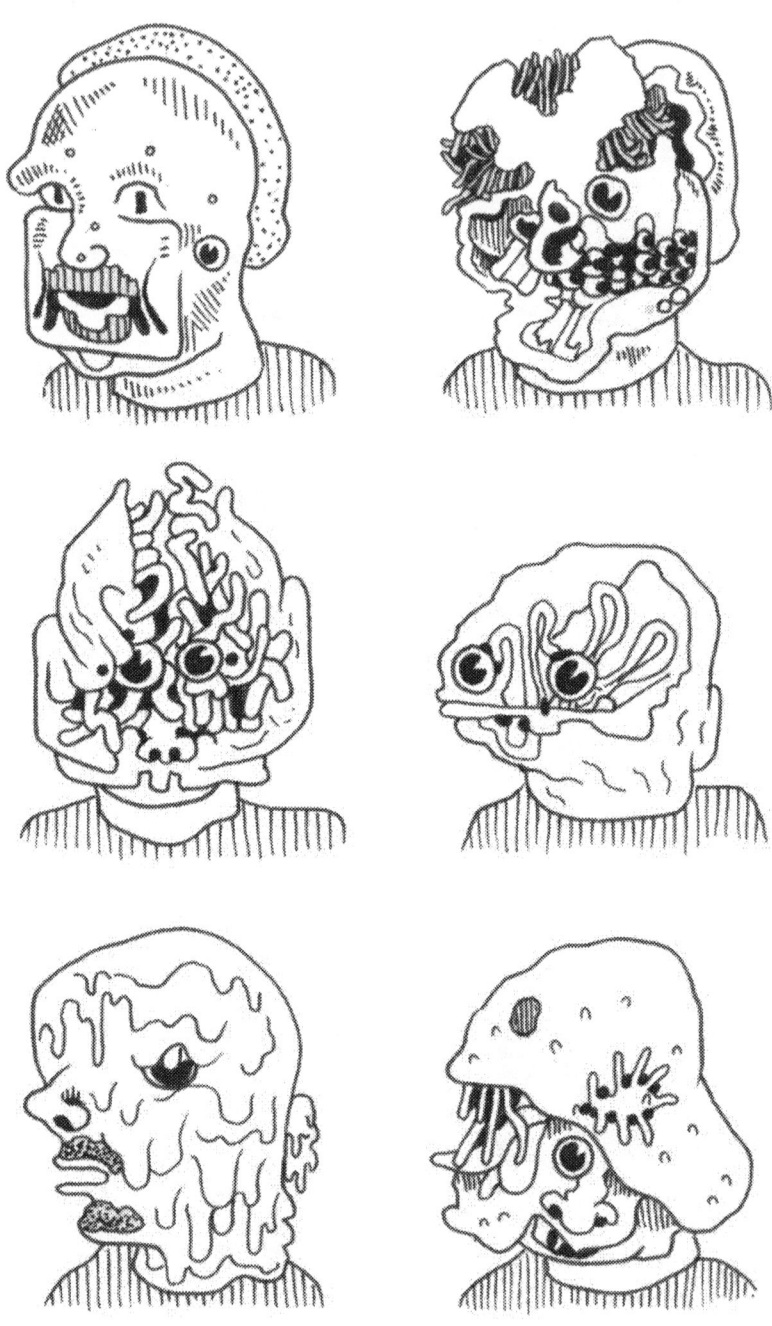

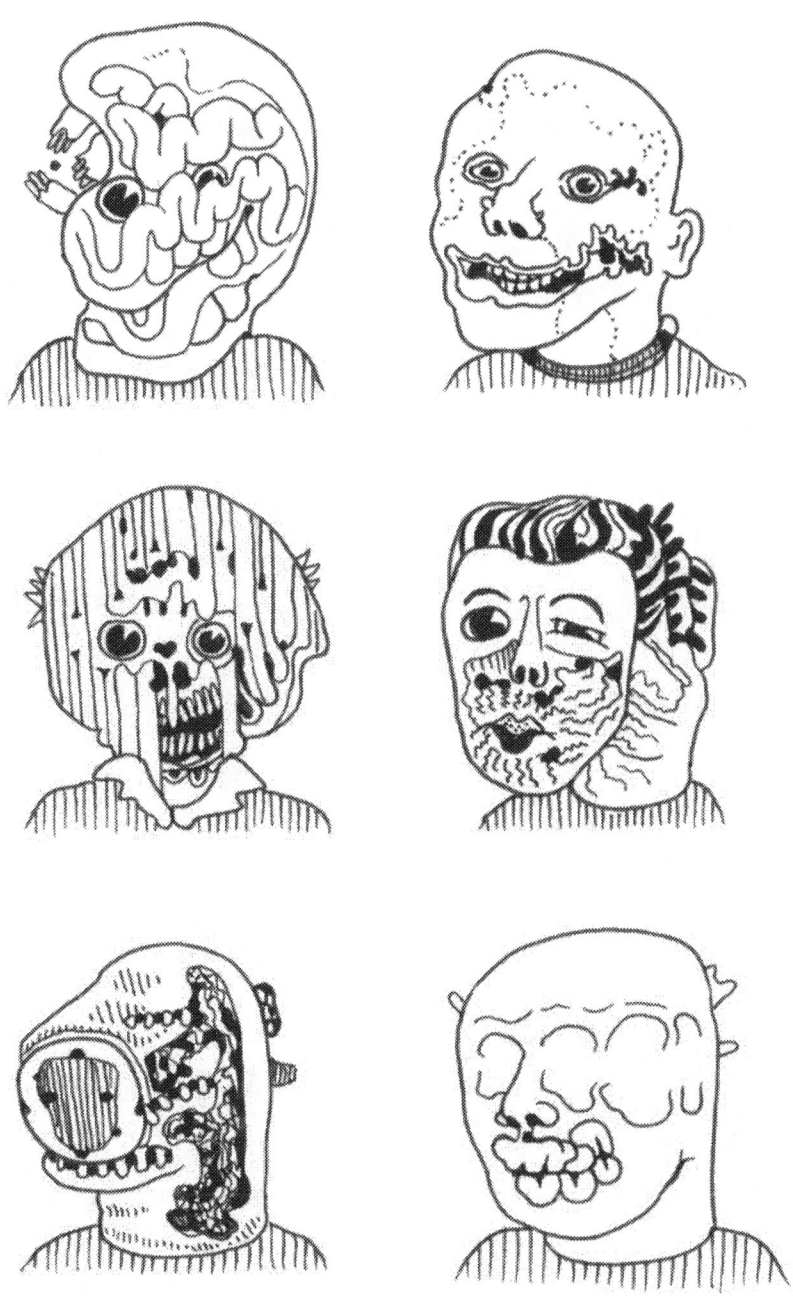

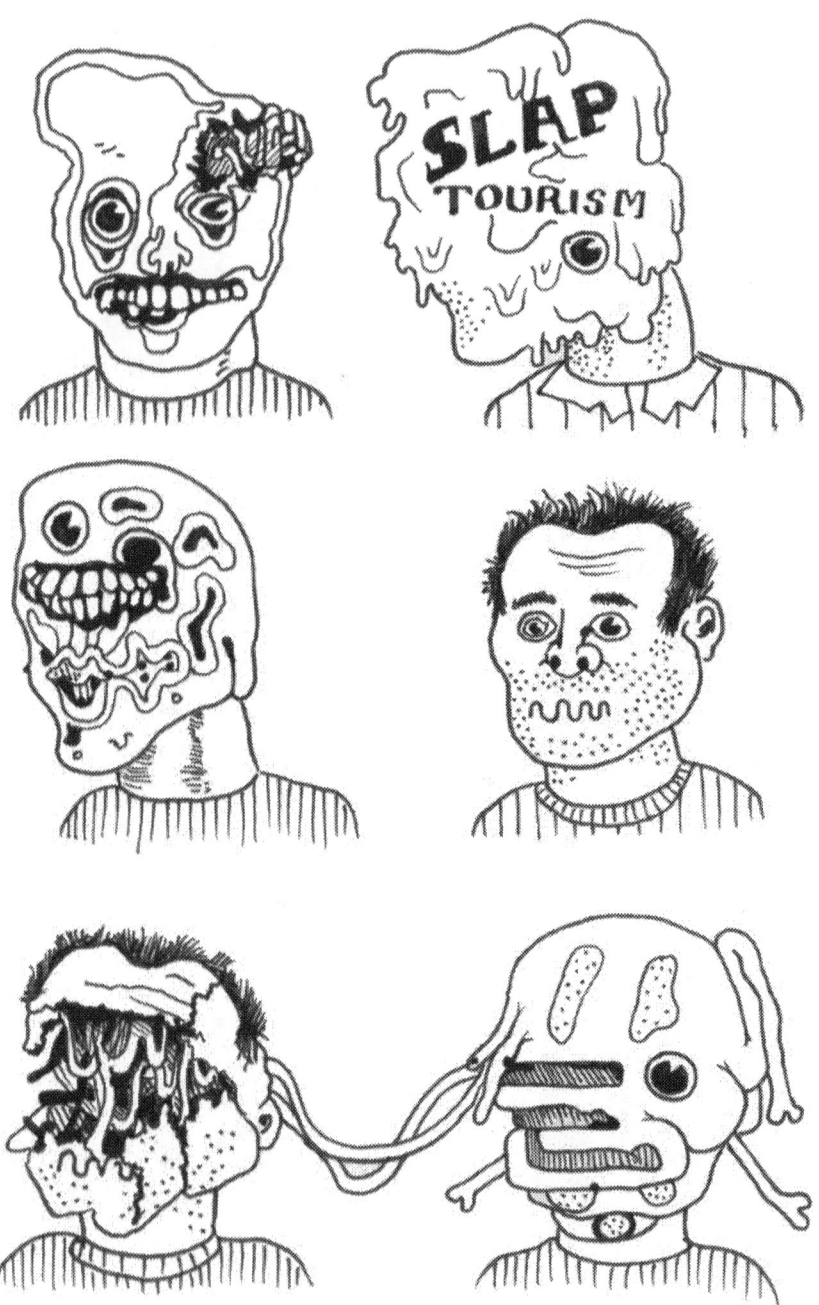

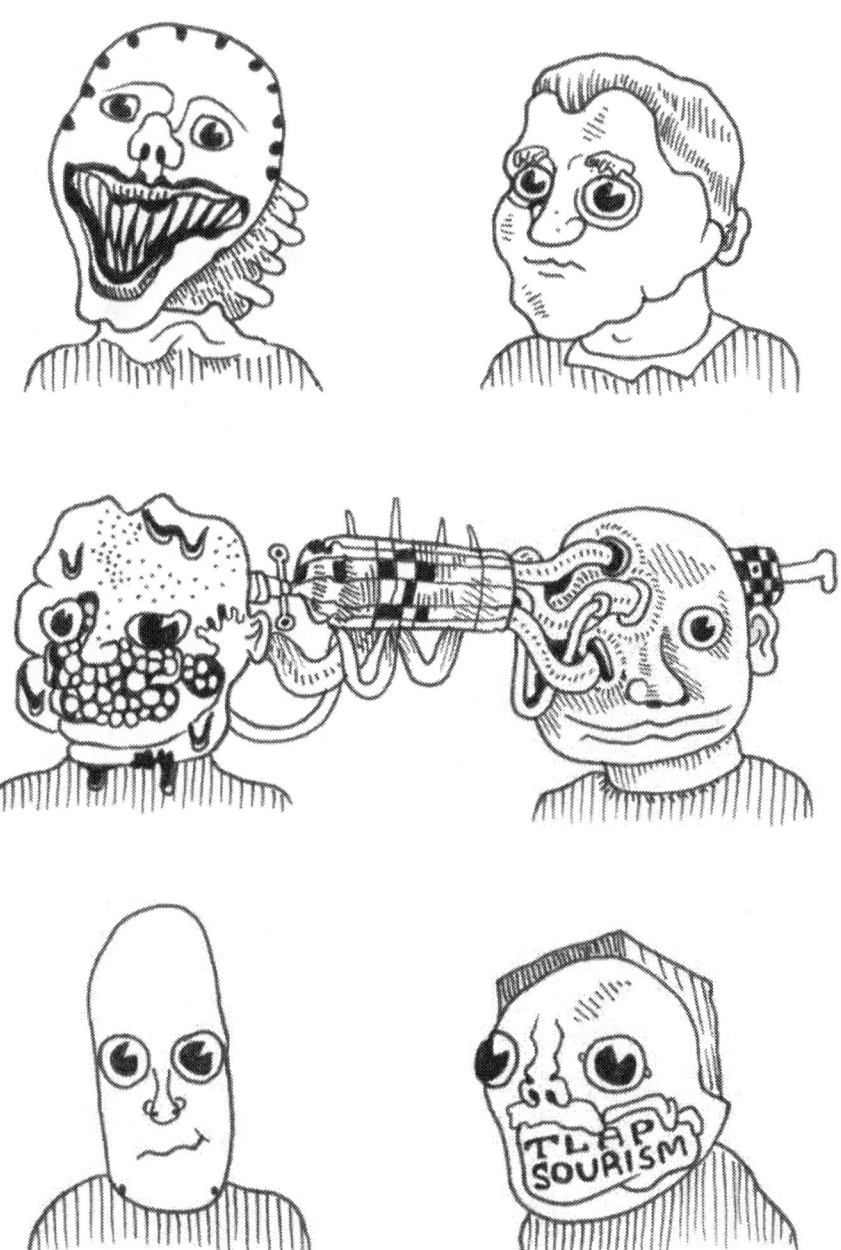

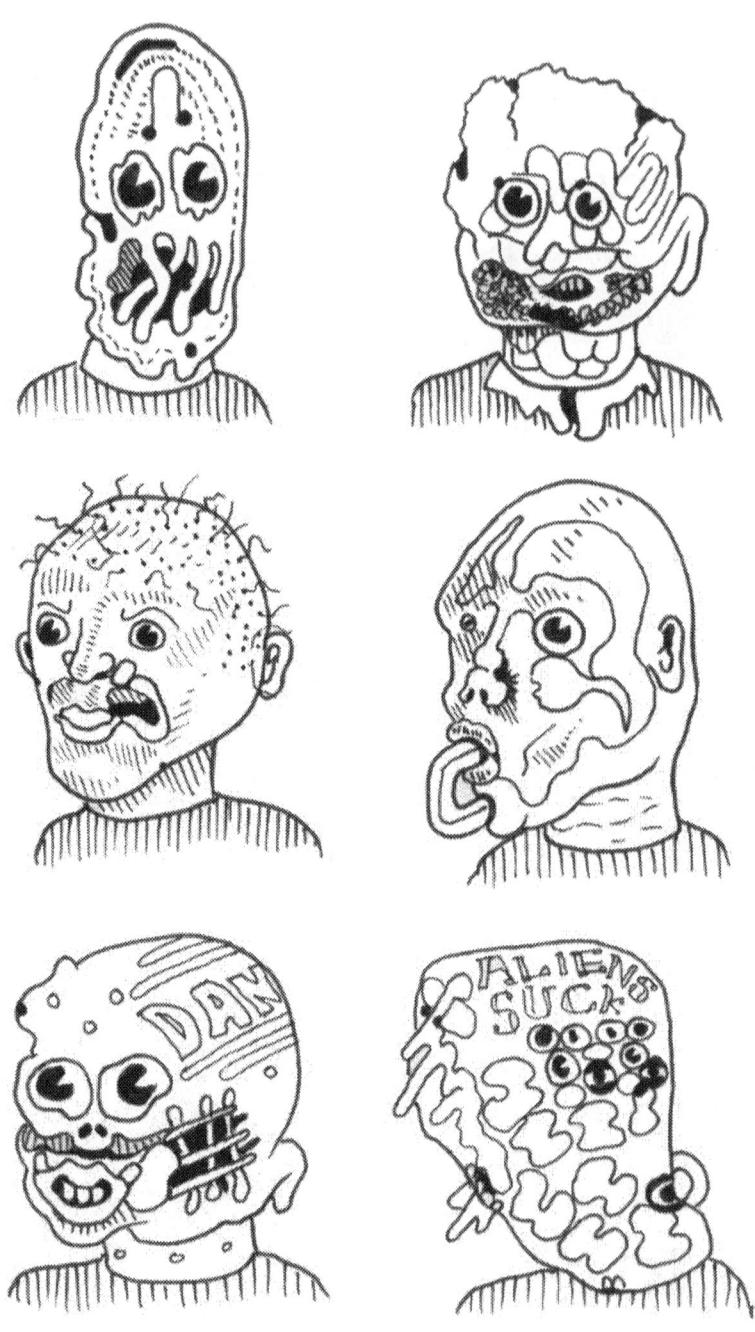

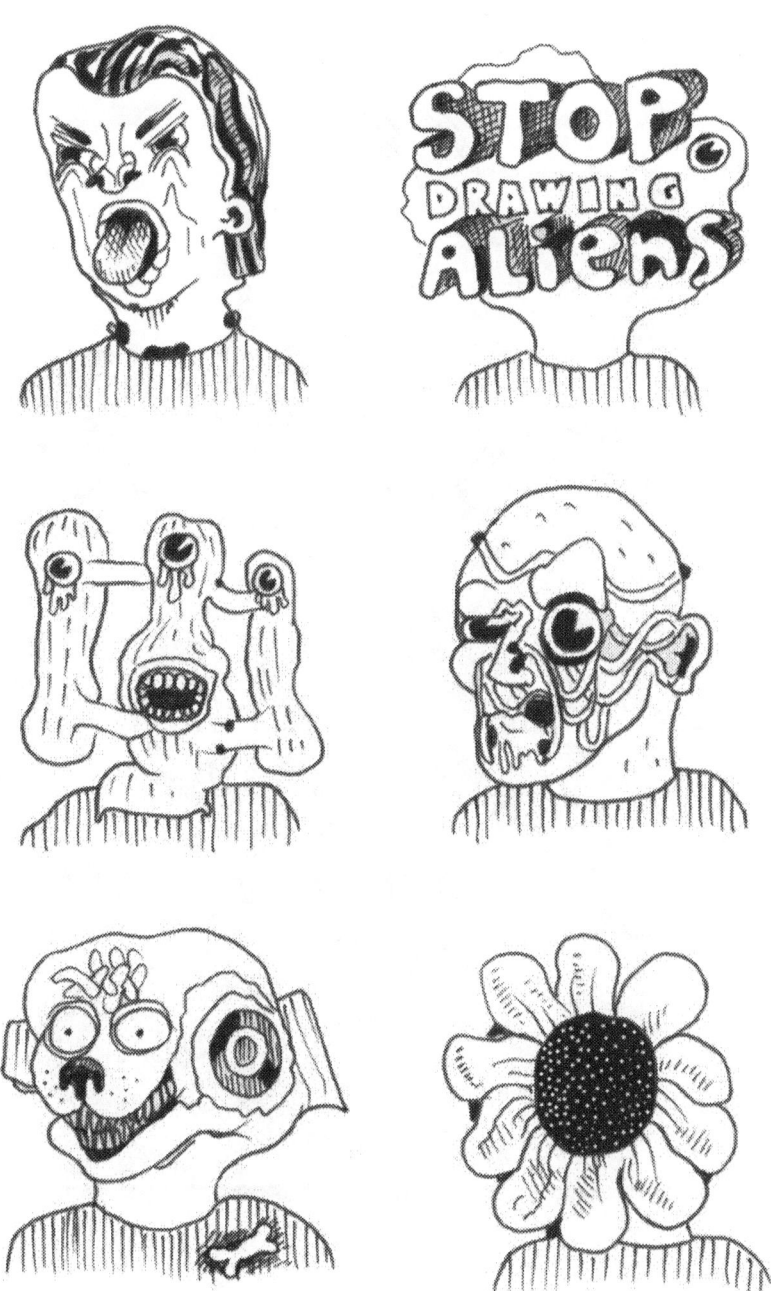

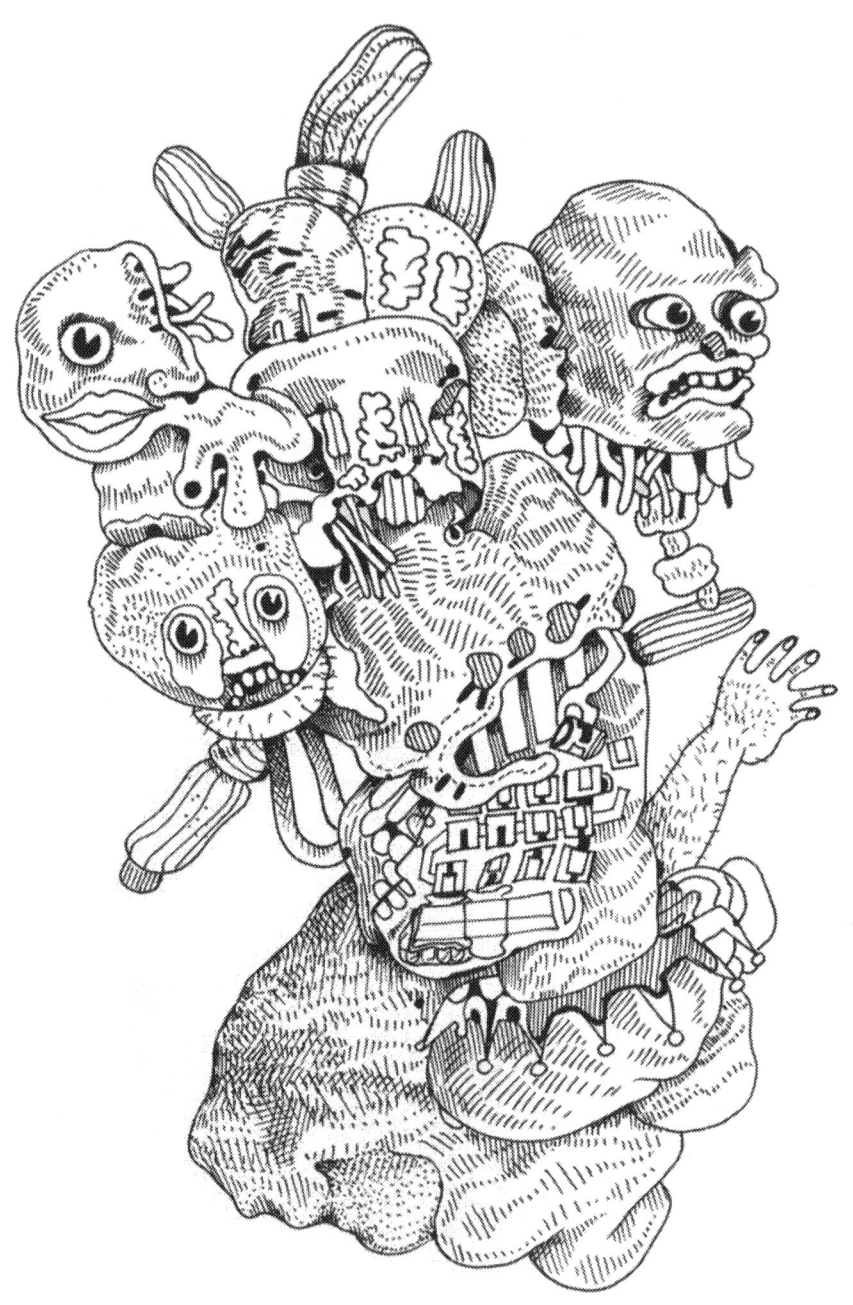

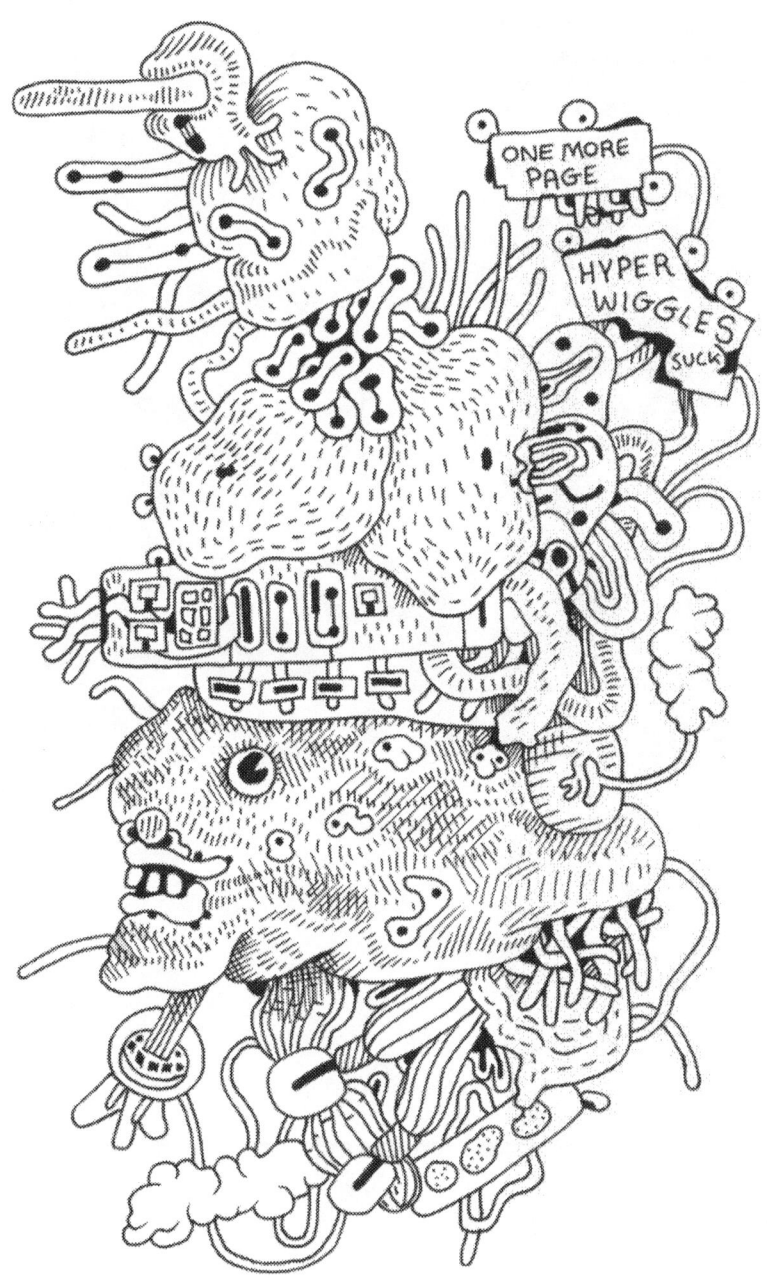

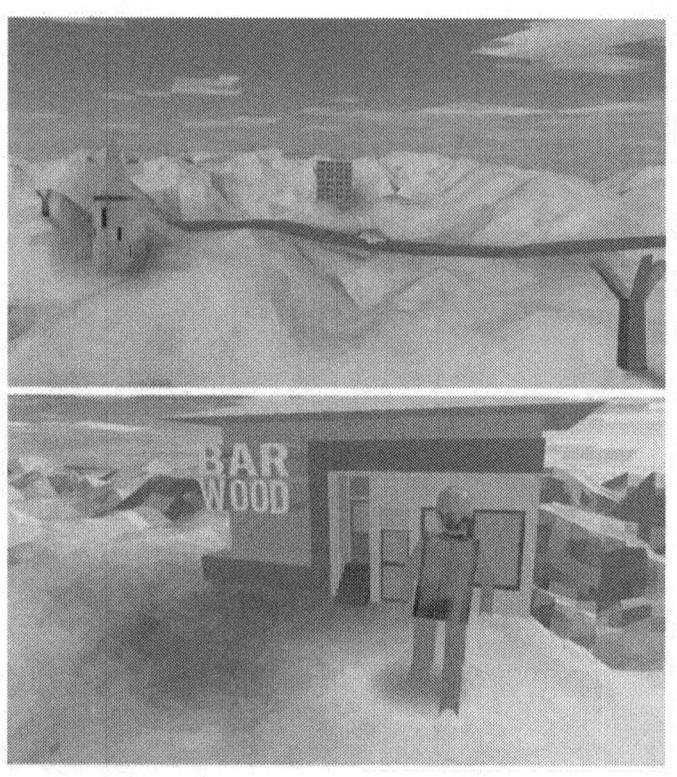

Mezlo's Trick - animated short, 2006

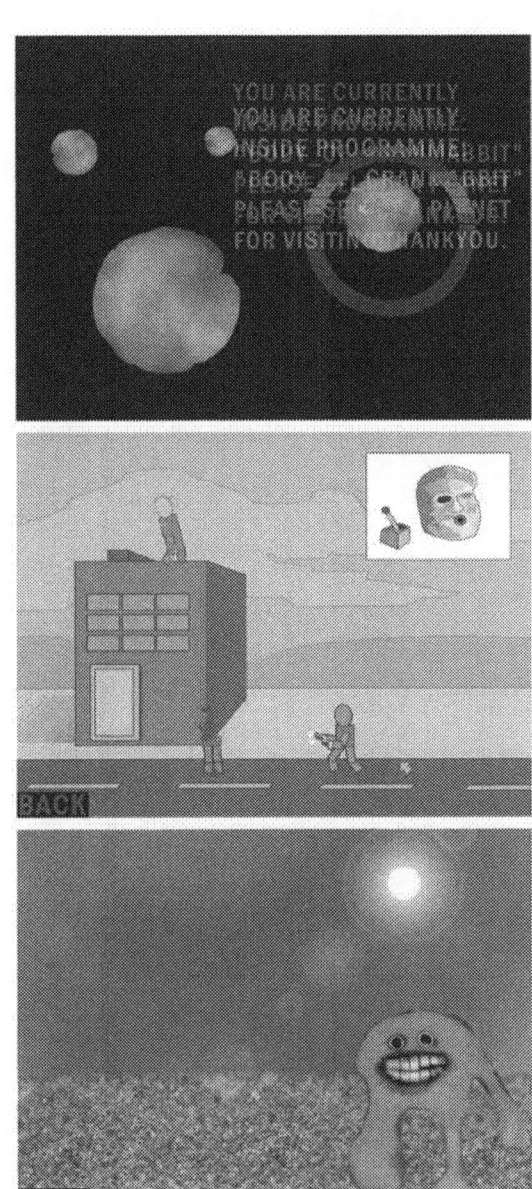

Cran Mabbit - computer game, 2005

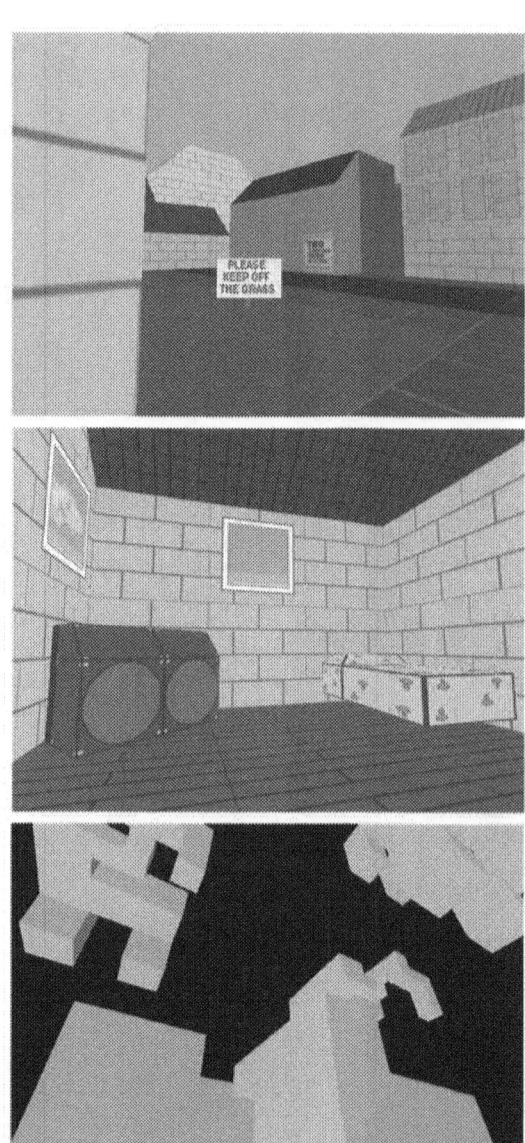

Mixing Woods - computer game, 2006

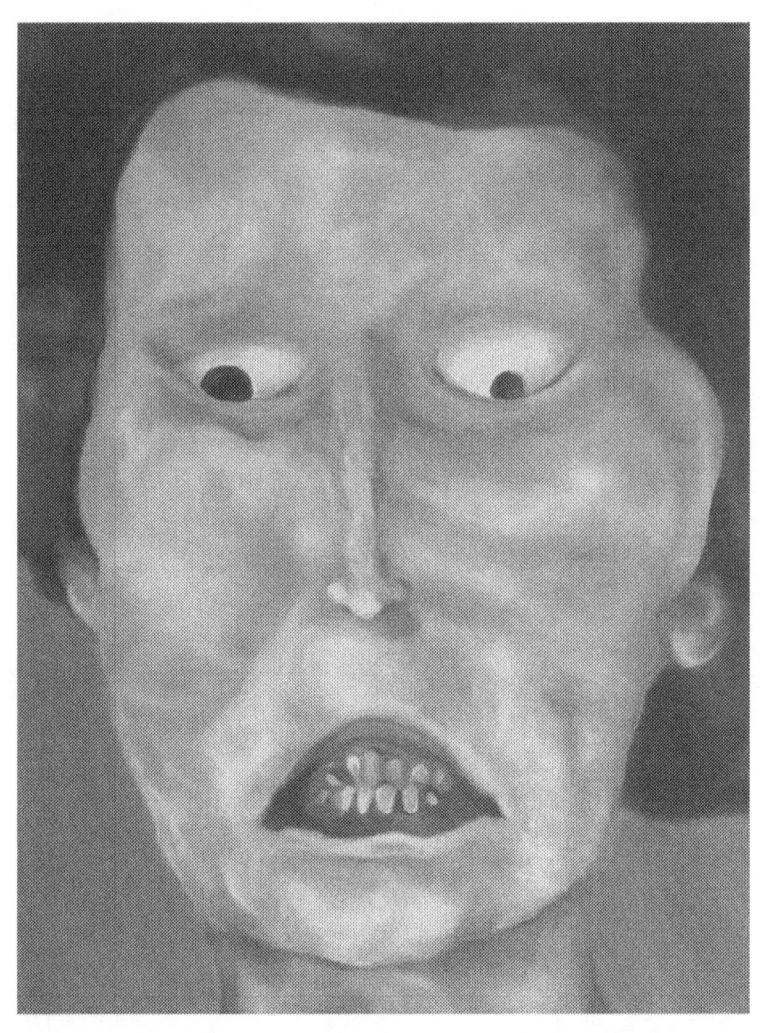

Long titles are really cool because they can be self-referencing and make me look like I know what I'm doing, 2005

(Alternative Title: Horrible Music)

250EZ

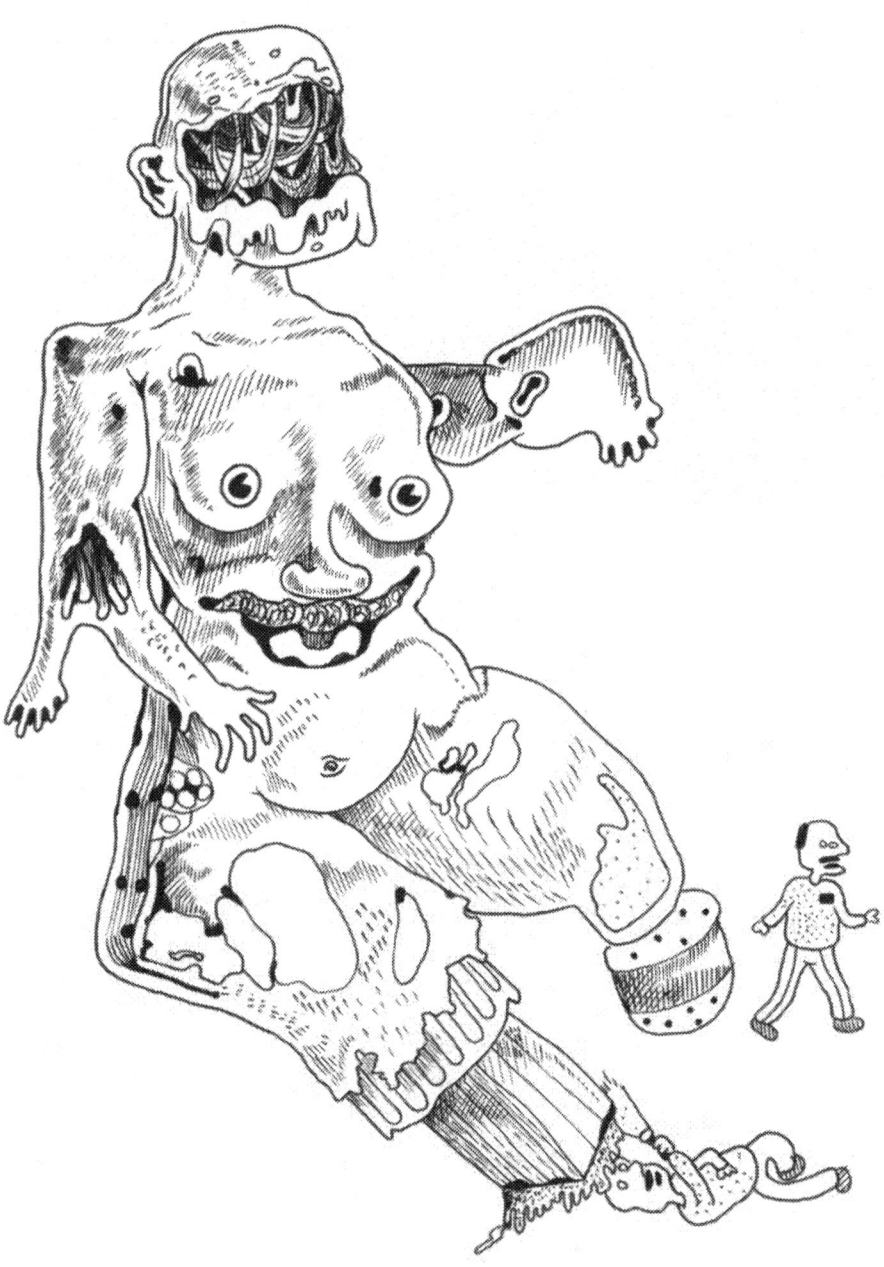

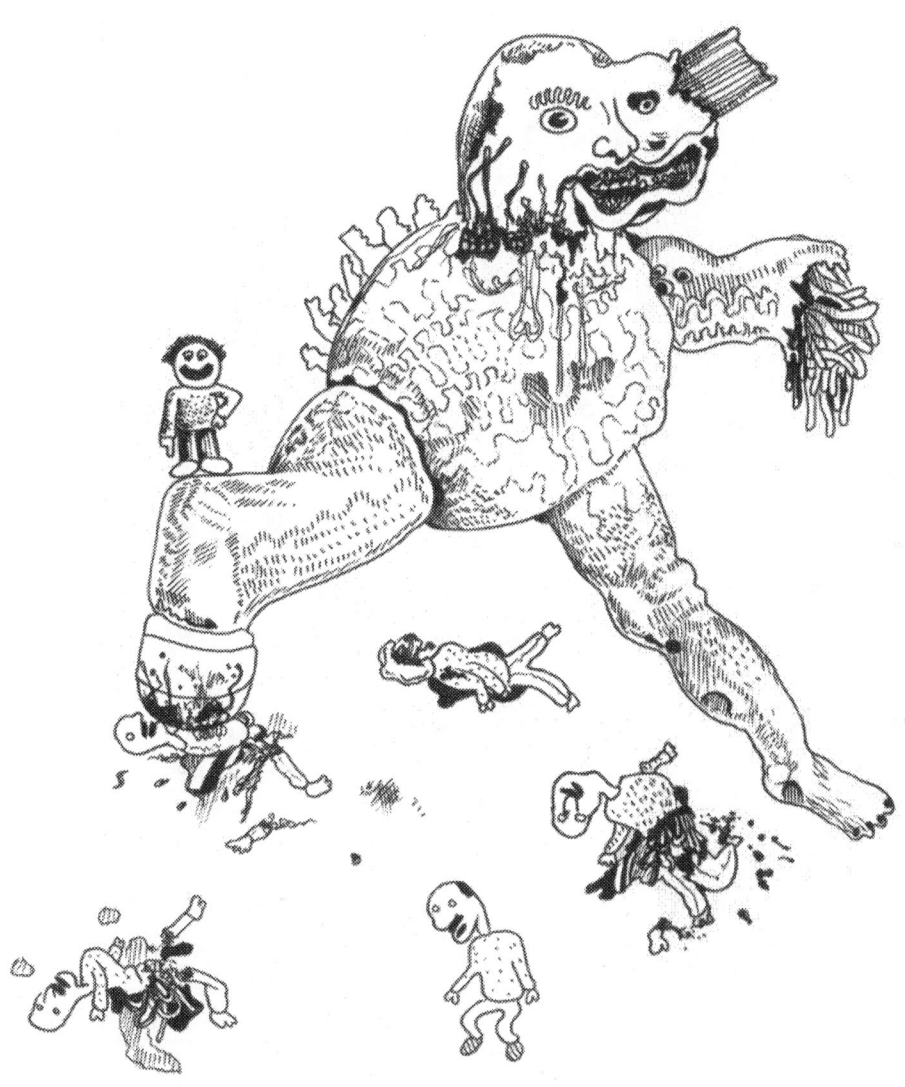

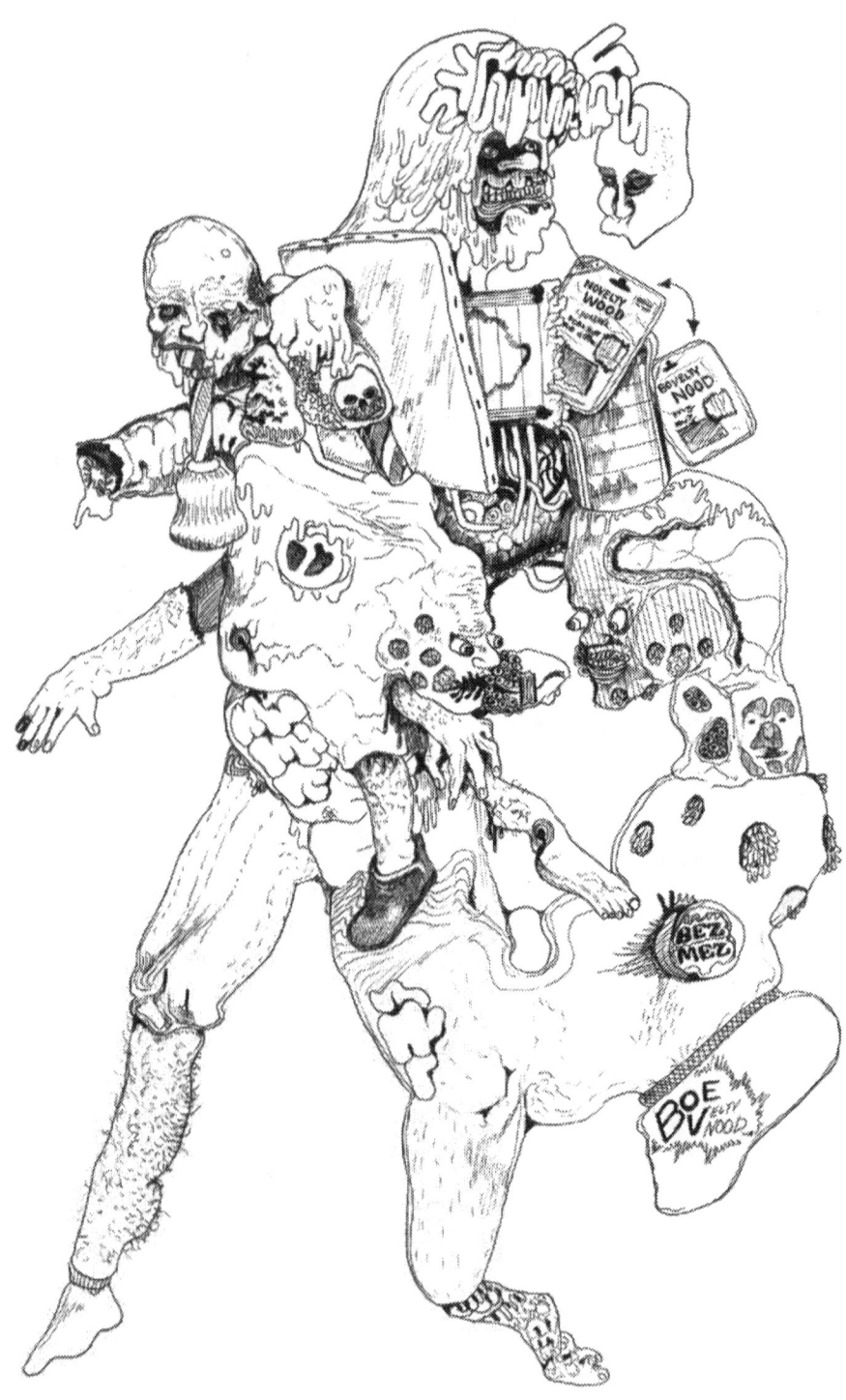

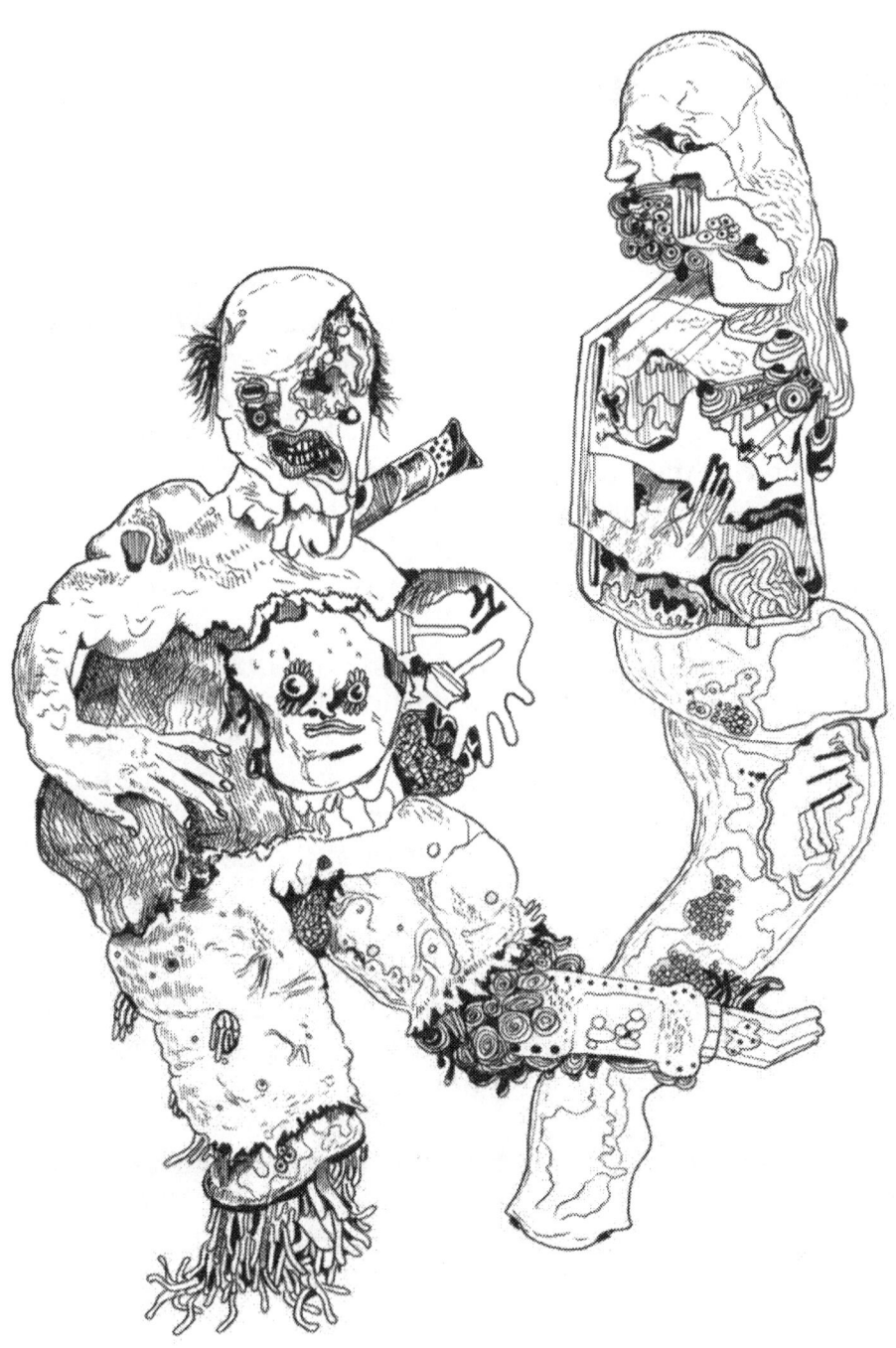

Andy Warhol

Introduction

Andy Warhol was an artist who was best known for his pop art and I want to look at this because I really like it. Andy Warhol was often known as "bombs Warhol" because of his love of bombs and what bombs are he used big bombs but in small room and recored the sound of the bomb explding from a tiny tube in a the room, so that it made a sound like a pop, which is where the name pop art comes from.

The colours in this piece are typical of pop art because they are colourful and andy warhol often used these type of painting colours because when they exploded next to bombs they made bits of canvas with colour on "spray out everywhere into fine little ribbons" I like this piece because it is really colourful and creates a vivid sense of strikeing colour in it - colourful.

In a quote from andy warhol he says " I used to use bangers a lot because they are swell and remind me of little bombs really – yet my desire for bigger bombs required me to seek out much more powerful explosives, I really like bombs. I'm Andy Warhol" I think this illustrates that rather than british art at that same time(1980s), which was mostly about trapping animals and   trapping animals, amercan art, (and warhol was amercan) was more about bombs

'bombs' Warhol and his rise to fame

the first major exhibition that andy warhol had was in june of 1967 which was influenced by abstract expressionism and how it could be used to create clothing if instead of doing abstract expressionism, the artist instead makes clothing.
He said in an interview:

[warhol]...eventually I want to make something with more pop...

[interviewer:] or bang?

[warhol] yeah actually that's an impressive idea because clothes don't bang much

[interviewer:] when you mention clothes, are you referring to the recent abstract expressionist movement?

[warhol] yeah, although , lol, I should probably actually be using bombs instead of clothes

[interviewer:] well why not?

[warhol] OMG ur a genius!

Most critics agree that is is where warhol got his idea for using bombs from,

INTERVIEW WITH BEN WHEELE

from 'nonsense art analysis'

Kel: Ben, what is slap culture?

Ben: Well imagine being slapped really hard and then watching some TV. Probably that is it.

Kel: That's a bit of a dead-end answer isn't it? How can people understand your work if you are going to reply so flippantly to questions? Do you not want people to understand your work?

Ben: Okay sorry, that was a pretty bad definition. Think back into time, there was once this thing called 'painting well' and a whole wealth of knowledge on how you perform this thing. Artists then gradually challenged it, painting in ways which people thought was not painting well (a classic is Picasso) and the artists knew that they weren't traditionally 'painting well' too, but they still painted. Actually today we think these look pretty good because our perceptions have changed and stuff and these have become the accepted ideas on how to 'paint well'. Next in queue we have post-modernism – a sort of cheeky, ironic reflecting on things, whereby any sources are game to create new things – you can reference anything now! It's madness! Andy Warhol referencing tins of soup? Absolutely crazy! The Simpsons referencing itself?? But it wasn't crazy; well not really, the references were (and still largely are) things which have 'appeal' and things which enough people will 'get' and 'notice' so as to make it pleasing and valid.

Slap culture is almost 'badly done post-modernism'. So, for example the referencing of something seen on telly 5 minutes ago, or self-referencing to the point of it becoming boring and stupid and not 'working' at all. Or the satire of a thing that nobody believes in and isn't in a powerful position anyway. These aspects make it quite hard to understand perhaps – what is he referencing? Why has he mentioned this thing 'Novelty Wood' and what does Henry eat? But if you understand Slap aesthetics, you might realise that you don't really *need* to understand slap aesthetics.

62

Kel: Hmm okay so basically everything you do is valid and good, no matter what people say because it's 'slap culture'. Ben that's a bit brash isn't it? The work seems to me to be just this arrogant geeky 'boys club art' that is *always* right no matter what people say about it.

Ben: Oh, well I think the main problem here is that I made Slap Culture sound good and valid, it's not. Do you want me to defend my work? I can if you want me to, we can play that game, it's fun, but first consider something – the language I just used – did you notice it? I said 'do you want me to "defend" my work'. When talking about arguments we almost always use 'war' language:

'The union *won* the argument over wages and have stopped striking.'

'Moley *attacked* the claims *against* him.'

If we together realise that these war-like win or lose metaphors lie deeply within individualist traditions of the self, then we may be able to approach arguments in different ways – after an argument nobody 'came off worse' but instead perhaps we 'both explored' a certain area or idea. Thereby establishing a more relationally productive approach.

Kel: Okay... but still, though, you are doing the same thing again, making up a scenario so that whatever people say against your work, you are always right and they are wrong.

Ben: listen to your own language! 'Whatever people say *against* your work' – you are assuming that there is some objectively accurate 'good' and 'bad' art that is the truth and it is reality. People have made it into truth, and therefore it becomes reality. But it's nonsensical – even to say that art is 'just opinions' doesn't make sense, it is an oxymoron, for opinions are learned from the rules of certain games, and develop over time to create new paradigms and rules.

Kel: All right, I can see we're not going to get anywhere along this argument. How do you feel that your—

Ben: ---where were we trying to get?

Kel: Sorry?

Ben: you said we were not going to 'get anywhere' along the current argument. Where were we trying to get?

Kel: well, to something that makes sense,

Ben: riiiiight...

Kel: So basically, you create this inclusive little fantasy world with its systems and things, and then come up with some wordy arguments to support it?

Ben: support it from what... becoming bad art? I already told you, Slap culture isn't good or valid. It is flawed like a rotten apple yet it appears a perfectly formed apple from the outside. I use pleasing aesthetics because I like them personally. I'm not interested in this noble 'act', which lots of artists play, where they pretend that 'things which look good' aren't really very sublime and are really unfashionable and commercialised– so things like sunsets in postcards and Salvador Dali are double-hyper anti-sublime and unfashionable. Yet, despite this... even minimalism was aesthetically pleasing – art cannot hide from aesthetics since art can be anything, and nothing in this world looks particularly 'ugly' - just different. If you call it art, it looks good, not the other way around.

Kel: do you like Salvador Dali?

Ben: to be honest, I don't really like any 'art' except for my own because I made it. I can appreciate other artwork totally, but I don't 'like' it in the way that I feel I should. A classic example is Eric Gill's work. I used to find it really sickly and just type-fonts and awkward naked women carved in stone, but after watching a TV programme on him, and learning that he practiced bestiality within 500 meters of where I live (Ditchling Common), and that he was fiercely incestuous, yet incredibly religious and that the residents of Ditchling aren't actually that proud that he lived in their quaint little village, despite all of his fame. All of those aspects made me quite like his artwork, because he has become interesting to me. It doesn't mean I'd want to carve artwork that looks like Eric Gill's, but if I *was* Eric Gill then I would do. I'd certainly buy a piece by him for my bedroom – I'd buy the etching of a naked Jesus descending from heaven, fully excited downstairs (if you know what I mean...)

Kel: I doubt very much that you are going to be a successful artist – if that's what you want (it sounds like it is) and I doubt very much that this 'pre-career monograph' is going to be popular too. While it is in my mind, the whole 'pre-career monograph' thing – just another classic Ben Wheele *'look at how eccentric and crazy I am'* stunt, isn't it?

Ben: I'm not eccentric...I'm not crazy...

Kel: Typical. I knew you were going to say that - you just can't be wrong can you?! You won't ever accept defeat...

Ben: I am wrong! I'm always incorrect!

Kel: aargh! Stop it! You're so *annoying* - your artwork?? it's a puddle of immature, meaningless bad arguments... (and don't even get me started on your poorly informed idea of art-history...)

Ben: It's not artwork...

Kel: *rolling eyes* Oooh I'm so scared...So was this all just one big self-reflexive piece of art?

Ben: afraid so! Right! I'm off to go and get mugged now, see-you later alligator.

NORMAL

- Kissing   • Shopping   • T.V.

- Hands   • Doctors   • Blond Hair   • Brown Hair

- Gold   • Legs   • Money

- Poverty

- Shoes   • Friends

- Lists   • Running

- Sunglasses   • Being similar to David Shrigley

- Scott Joplin

- Police   • Children   • Classical Music

- Treble   • Bass

- My Piano

- Spiders   • The olden days   • Fruit

- The word 'Wiggling'   • Palm trees

- Mr. Darcy   • Hope

- The Tate Modern   • Dentists

- Things getting 'broken'   • Pretending to be 'not normal'

- Assorted fundamentalists

- Goldsmiths college   • The internet

NOT NORMAL

- 'Lenny' backwards (ynneL)   • Nin   • Tissue Jam

- 'Why are you smiling' Juice   • Whillugp

- Police-children who have ultimate power over the adult police

    • Golf   • Zez Confrey

- Jokes about Golf 'not being normal'

- Father-shoes   • Normal

- Billy Mayerl

- Mr.   • Yeah! From your tummy

- Wiggles

- Triple mistakes (double is better, though)

- Slap-terrorism   • being right

- Self-Reflexivity

- 'Mr. Poo' who refuses to ever change his name out of pride for his family and who defies social constraints in the touching 1930's abysmally amazing dance.

- The dinternet

- Rare collection Oats

- Monty Python's 'Rip-off of Ben Wheele' Flying Circus

- Beards (predictably 'not normal' things - yawn)

Artist Gavin Turk Sues Faeces

In a recent interview, artist Gavin Turk explains why he wanted to 'sue a poo' in the name of art
Jame Chran is interviewing, Jame Chran is a leading art critic of yeah

JC: so how legally did you pull this off? Surely any lawyer would disregard this as utter nonsense and tell you to go home

GT: you would think that, you *really* would, but it was fine, I hired a lawyer for a lot of money and he is helping me sue the poo, although he wishes to remain anonymous.

JC: what on earth are you suing it for?

GT: ahh that's part of the artworks mystery

JC: right... ok so who's faeces is it?

GT: I don't know I found it in the toilets unflushed, I was like "wow! Free art!"

JC: So all art is shit then?

GT: All shit is art!

JC: *laughs* so where did you get the idea from to do this?

GT: well originally (I'm dyslexic) I thought sue was spelt soo and I was going to make a book called "how to soo a poo". I then found out that they didn't rhyme and it spoiled it a bit, but I carried on anyway, regardless.

JC: sue and poo...they do rhyme...

GT: yeah but not properly

JC: well...yeah they do, properly...

GT: look you know I'm dyslexic after all so maybe they do rhyme but that's not the point,

JC: so what is this 'piece of art' - and I use the term loosely here Gavin, what is its point then?

GT: well...suing a poo

JC: ah ok, I get it now – wow it's actually incredibly touching and moving and...the more I think about it - a piece of resounding, stunning beauty!

GT: *smiles* thanks

The entire interview is available on audio disk it's really good.

Many proprietors of the main lobby eventually found it all quite heart warming – mainly because, indeed the word 'found' if it had to rhyme with anything, would probably rhyme with 'ground' or perhaps even 'round'. This was however put to vote; most people decided that it should be rhymed with 'lound', despite 'lound' not really being a common (or real) word.
Subsequently it was decided that a meaning should be generated for this word, lound. Many options were considered – firstly fingernail yeah not no yeah. No.
Secondly ringside champions who like to jump on the mats because they are a little bit springy. This was adopted because of this rhyme: -

"what sport is this where no lound is found a-jumpy?"

The popular rhyme dates back to the year 1865. Interestingly, this was written in June. Which day in June? November. Many people still believe November to be another month, BUT IT CAN BE USED AS A DAY!!!!1111 OMG! WHY DOESN'T ANYONE BELIEVE ME! Go and be another typical 'Goldsmiths' Contemporary Artist.

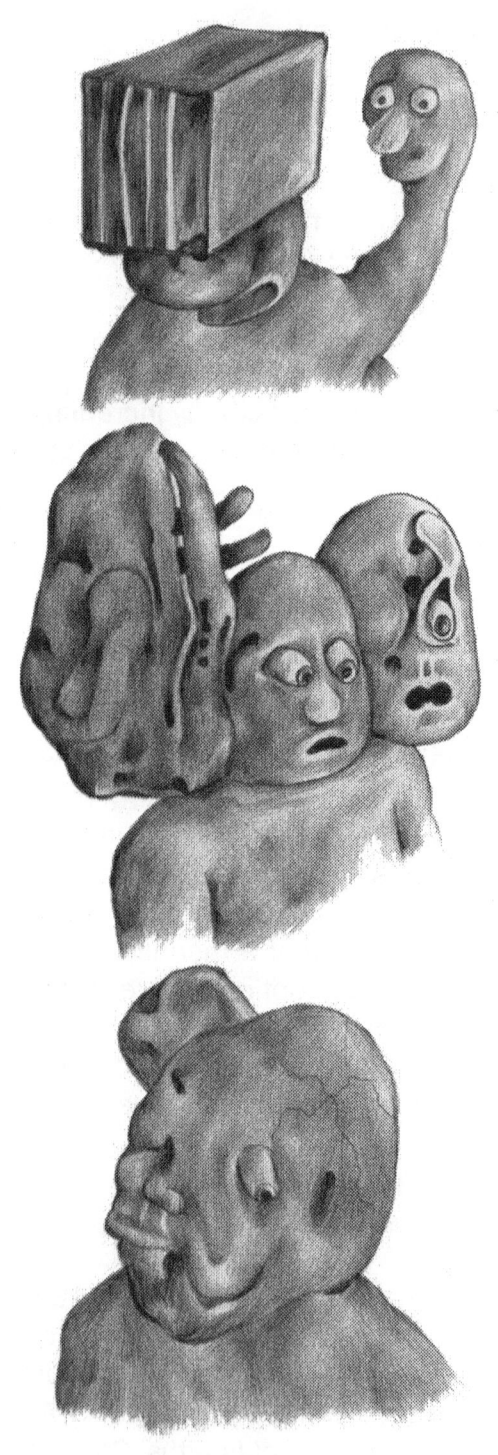

The wiggles were shocked and angry at Bens stupid idea for a project.

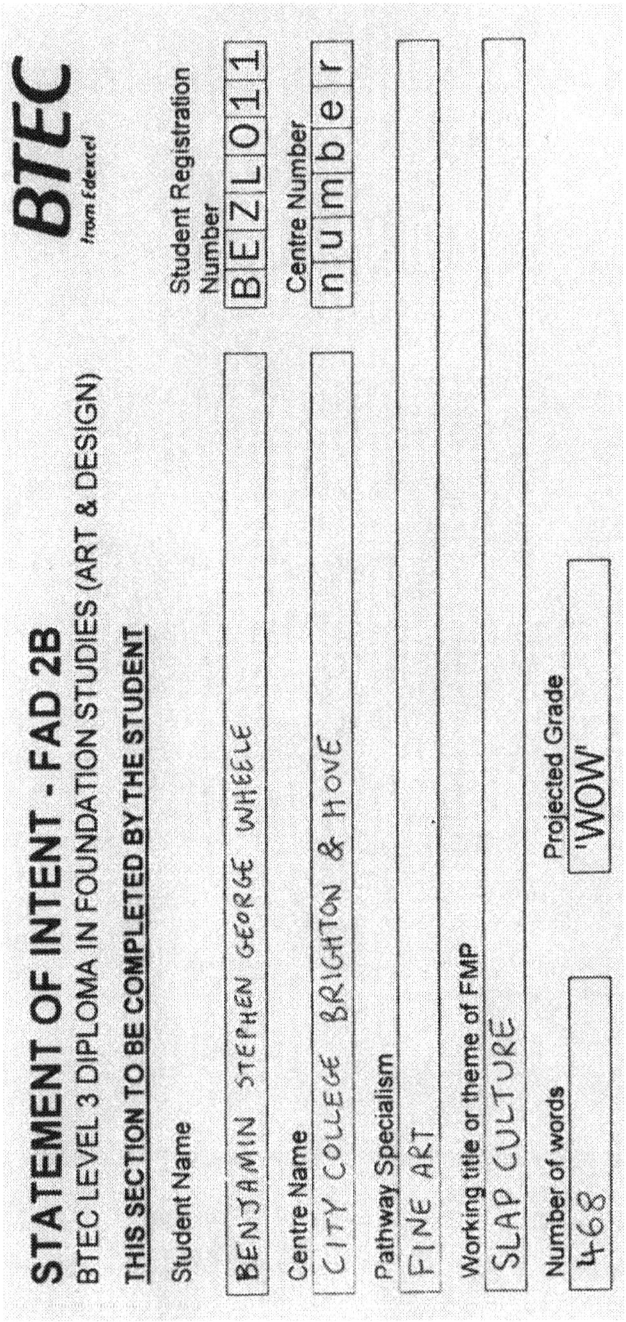

BTEC
from Edexcel

STATEMENT OF INTENT - FAD 2B
BTEC LEVEL 3 DIPLOMA IN FOUNDATION STUDIES (ART & DESIGN)

THIS SECTION TO BE COMPLETED BY THE STUDENT

Student Name

BENJAMIN STEPHEN GEORGE WHEELE

Centre Name

CITY COLLEGE BRIGHTON & HOVE

Pathway Specialism

FINE ART

Working title or theme of FMP

SLAP CULTURE

Number of words

468

Student Registration Number

B E Z L O 1 1

Centre Number

n u m b e r

Projected Grade

'WOW'

Ben was shocked and angry that somebody had stolen, taken or possibly just moved 'What Wood Is That?' - 'I'll get the armpit-face that did it.' he yelled.

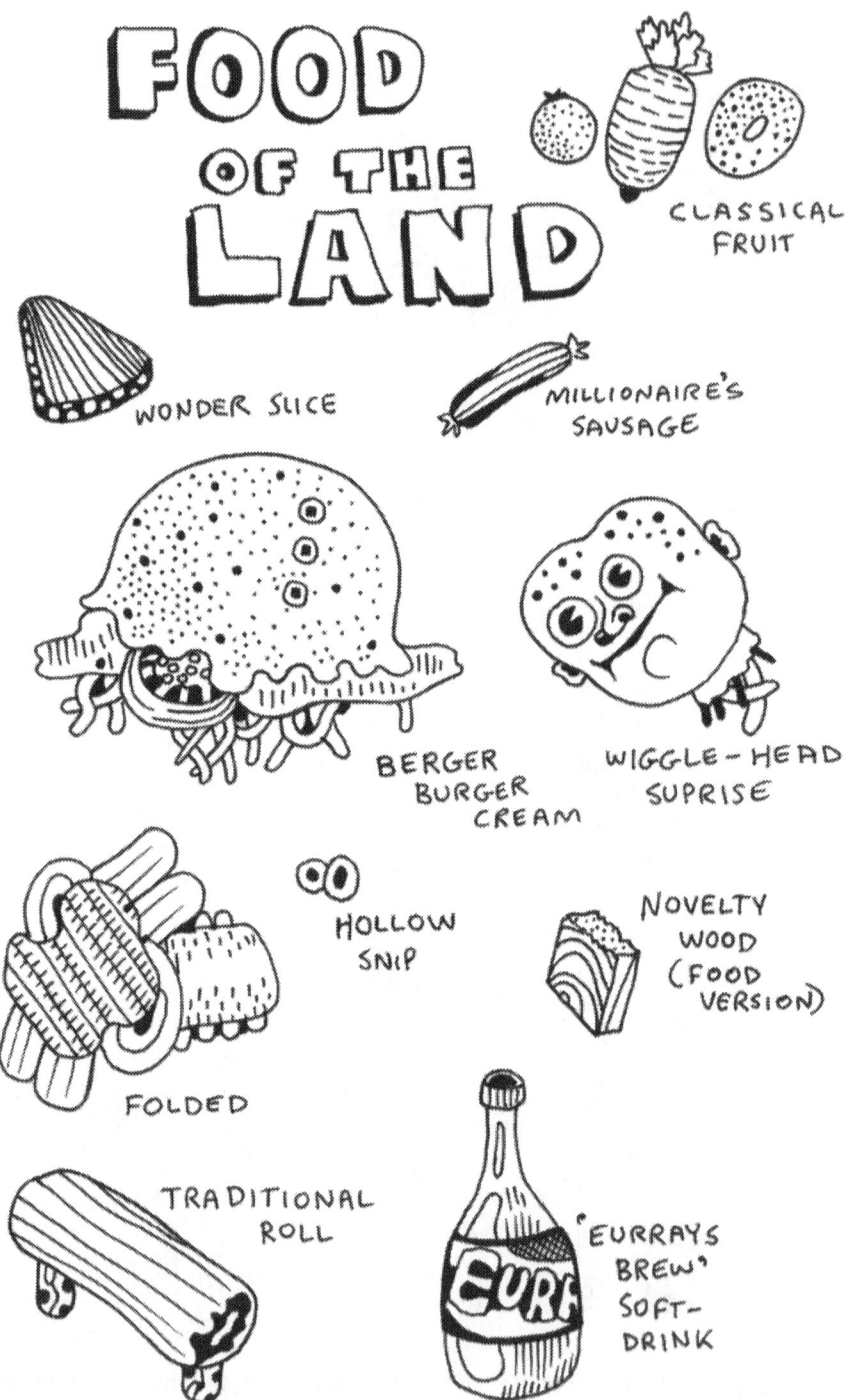

FOOD OF THE LAND

CLASSICAL FRUIT

WONDER SLICE

MILLIONAIRE'S SAUSAGE

BERGER BURGER CREAM

WIGGLE-HEAD SUPRISE

HOLLOW SNIP

NOVELTY WOOD (FOOD VERSION)

FOLDED

TRADITIONAL ROLL

"EURRAYS BREW" SOFT-DRINK

EURR

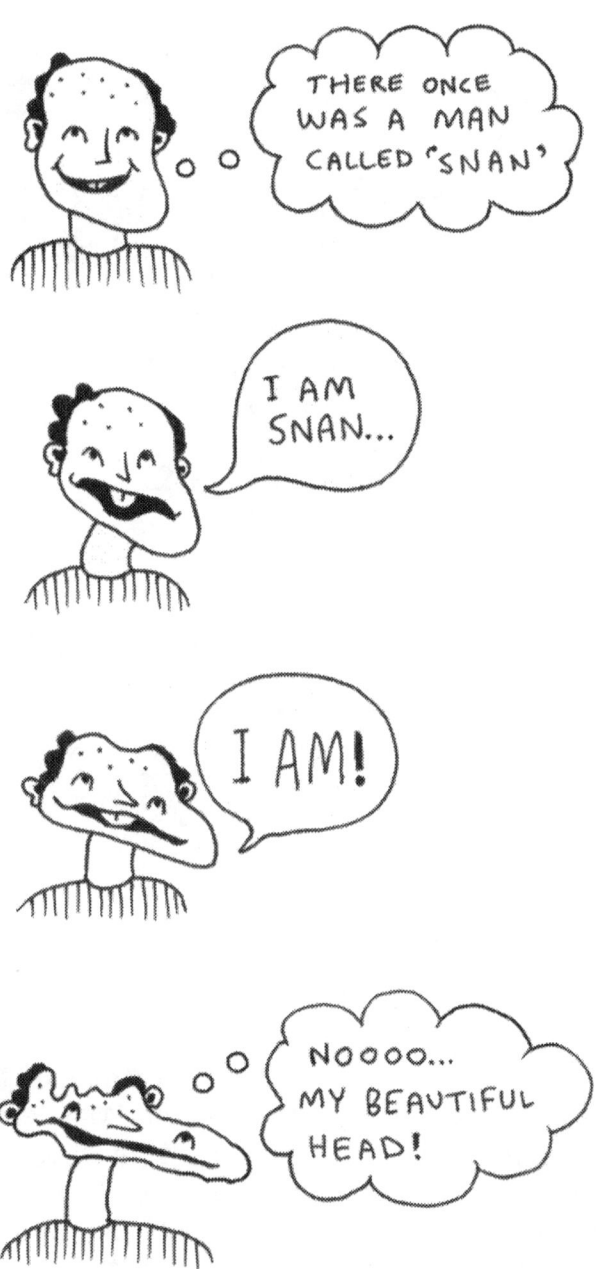

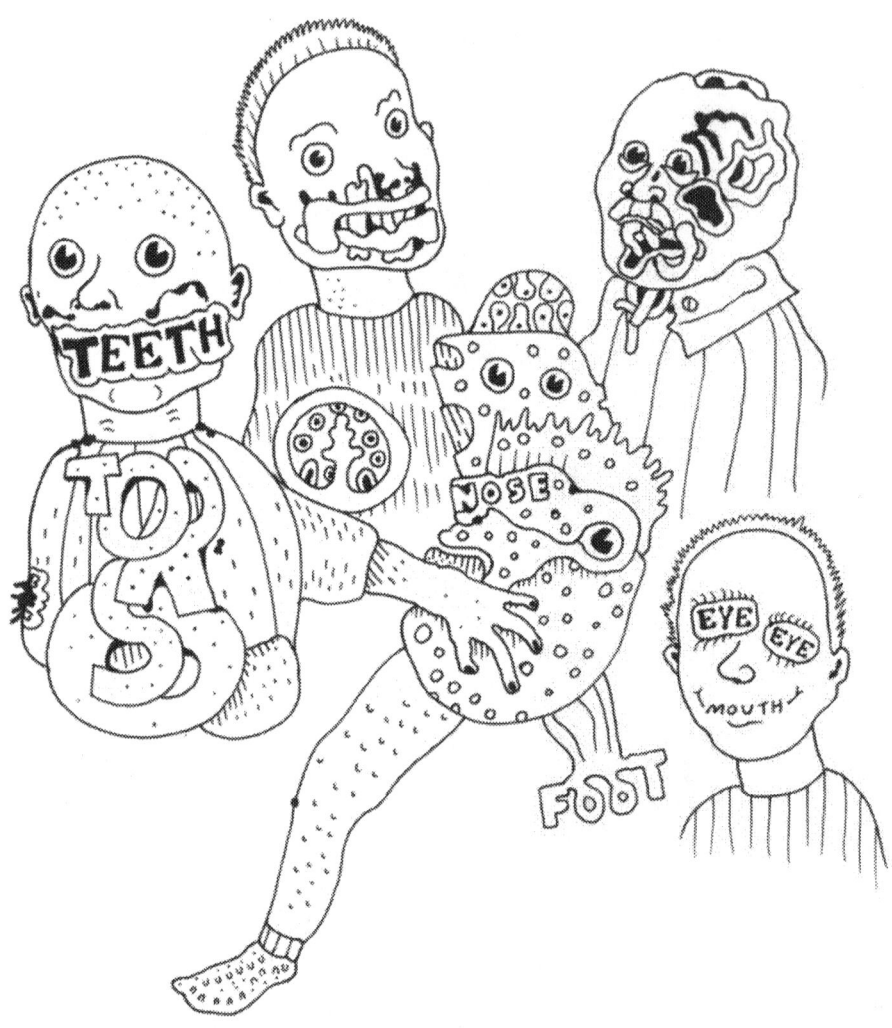

A wild family of working Wiggles stand in front of the camera-graph, ready to have their portraits taken. With teeth for teeth and eyes for eyes, they are now part of a cheap visual trick whereby words look slightly like the actual entities that they describe. Really *appalling*, if I am honest. So gloomy - (almost amazingly so) an idea, that it even made the cover two-piece down a gloomy cave where the wiggles work in underground factories and get eaten whenever. It's a utopia.

Joseph Simmonds on Novelty Wood

(see Fig.2 p77)

Ben Wheele is not in charge. Bezlo owns Novelty Wood. Bezlo connects to us through Ben Wheele from the world Ben wants to inflict upon us.

Novelty Wood is a means to an end. Yet the end is one we are not inclined to desire. We are used to products coming in packaging. We can exist because of the products that fulfil our needs. Of course there too exist things, which have this packaging that we do not need; yet we want them. Novelty wood appeals to our recognition of this packaging and we see Novelty Wood not as an art piece but as an art consumable. The 'Novelty' rules out need, so it is a luxury item. But it is a useless lump of wood.

It has a flavour; are we to eat the wood? Remove the packaging and the object changes, its then not Bezlo anymore but a misunderstood external thing. Bezlo has absorbed our packaged products and made his own variety. For us to use the packaging as a disposable layer would seem most off, perhaps even upsetting to Bezlo. To Bezlo what we see as packaging and product it sees as one thing.

To an extent Bezlo, which includes Novelty Wood, is Ben Wheele's filter for the world in which most of us reside. To Ben Wheele whether or not this is healthy is irrelevant, for he will see 'healthy' as a social construction.

Novelty Wood is intended for sale through vending machines and from shops, most likely newsagents, as a product on a mass-produced scale by poor people in Taiwan or Viet Nam. The inventor of Novelty wood says he finds it hilarious that the people usually producing a product that serves westerners with a use would be packaging and inspecting small pieces of purposeless wood.

As a label, if labels are necessary, what should we call Novelty wood? As a packaged object it most likely feels like sculpture, yet the vending machines, are they an extension of this? It's most probably best to view the whole of Novelty wood as a performance conducted by the consumers of the inconsumable wood; implemented by Bezlo through Ben Wheele.

There is no irony in the expected sense. Irony wasn't an influential feature in conceiving Novelty Wood. But it has become ironic from a sales point of view in the sense that a product has been made which doesn't do anything. It only serves as art. It's not a product that doesn't work, but one that isn't meant to. It works as art. And that is all.

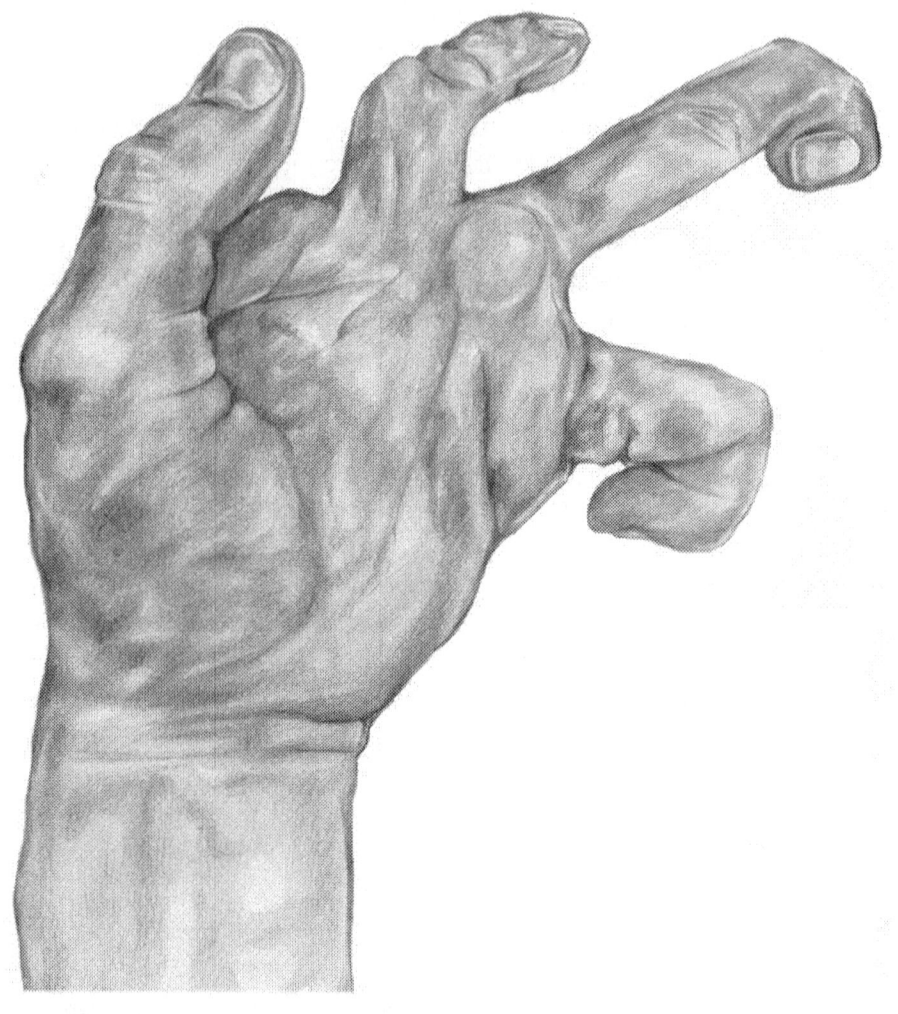

Fig.1 - 'Wiggle-Hand' also known as 'Greed-Fingering'

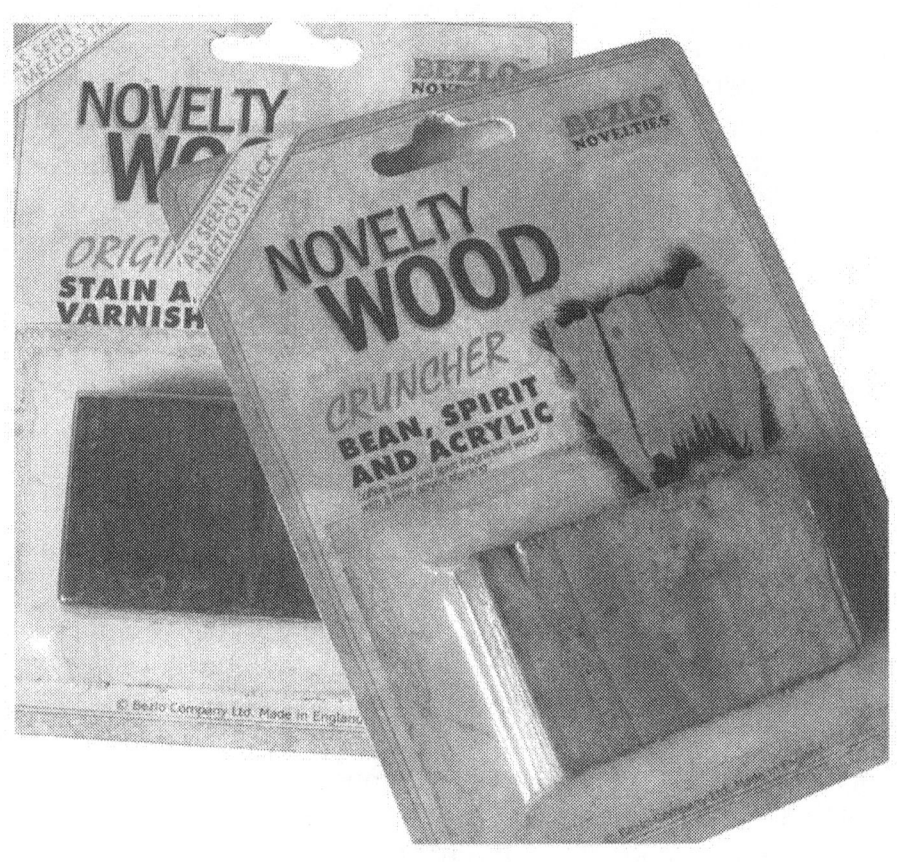

Fig.2 - Novelty Wood, 2006 stock

Show and Trell

Grey had been waiting here for ages, and the plastic seat he was sitting on had just entered into the realm of discomfort. What made it worse was his inability to stand up or stretch - he was strapped down by large metal bars (for his own safety, mind). Yet this discomfort was only noticed by his buttocks and only noticed subconsciously - for Grey had other more pressing issues to ponder whilst he waited.

Another four minutes passed before the ride began to clank. Grey could hear the mechanisms of the pulley system begin to warm up.

'Here I go!' Grey said aloud - even though he was sitting on the ride alone. It seemed that the excitement had begun to bubble up from his intestines and was now infecting his mind. The ride made a jud forwards and then stopped momentarily.

'What's gone wron...' Grey began to think, but before he could finish, the ride spurted into motion, moving him forward at a delightfully steady pace.

'Weeeeee!' exclaimed an overjoyed Grey.

The first room that the ride entered was from the legendary computer game 'Mixing Woods' (see p54). He appeared to be outside, in a vibrantly coloured small town. The smell of cherries was overwhelming and there was so much for Grey to see here! A group of leg warblers (people who walk horizontally) passed him to his left - their nighttime bodies thrashing about in a fury of loud warbling noises. Grey secretly still found this petrifying - even though he knew that they were perfectly harmless...weren't they?

The ride continued along the path, next to a wall. There was all manner of complimentary objects embedded in the wall here for passengers to take - however, small green slurpies and dog-willow nightmare holidays dominated these - of which Grey abhorred. Grey drew closer to a massive door that was decorated with all the pixels of the rainbow. It was so exciting! What could possibly be behind the door?

Before he could look around the next room, Grey was greeted by incredibly heavy gales, stinging at his face. He groped for his sunglasses. Admittedly, the warden had warned him about the wind in 'Room Two' yet Grey had declined his offer of wind goggles, thinking that he would be fine. Sometimes Grey was a bit stupid. The sunglasses sufficed to keep away the wind.

The room was built from dark stone, and the more Grey regained his eyesight, he realised that it wasn't a room at all - but a long narrow passage. Looking back, it was now impossible to see the door from which he had entered since he had travelled so far into the passage. A gentle sloping downwards was now noticeable, and with it came a gradual increase of speed. This sloping downwards was slowly increasing in its steepness, and for Grey this part of the ride was a little boring.

It was a time for some planning. When he reached the bottom (his destination of the 'Wiggles Factory') he wanted to be prepared with questions already, and not to just ask whatever entered his mind at that point - for he probably wouldn't have enough Ezlos to afford another ride here for another year (rhyme, Gavin!) so it was best to make the most of his visit.

Wiggles themselves are not good tour operators, since they are incredibly busy with their factory work. The arrangement is this - Normals (such as Grey) are as much dependent on the Wiggles as the Wiggles are dependent on the Normals. The relationship is reciprocal in the same sense that a bee's and a flower's is and the artist's with the art critic's (such as Kel). Wiggles can be eaten at anytime by a Normal, raw or cooked or whatever, and they don't mind this at all. They also produce power for the Normals using *trell*, which demands labour so hard, that even a minute of it would smash a Normal into tiny pieces. In return for their back-breaking work and open edibility, the Wiggles are permitted to set challenges for Normals - whatever they want, and the Normals must try their best to succeed in these, although they are not mandatory. The sheer presence of Normals and the opportunity for setting challenges excites and energises the Wiggles enough to inspire them into working for the Normals.

Grey recalled the last Wiggle challenge he was set - it was something about British soil and beavers, and even further back there was a challenge which involved other challengers, yet he couldn't quite recall who they were now, since it had been so long.

The descent was now very noticeably steep, and the wind had increased in velocity too. Grey's grip around the bars now tightened.

'I'm probably the bravest person I know...' Grey thought, 'Although sometimes I long for a person of whom appreciates this fact and, like a little Tarzan, looks up to me too and...'

The wind now screeched as Grey sped almost vertically downwards. The pressure on his sunglasses. It was too much. They smashed. Grey felt pieces of glass smatter over his face. His stomach felt like it was 10 meters above him as he. It was so windy and. It seemed so fast. On Wiggle Island. Is he? On Wiggle Island. Is he - he is on Wiggle Island. It's too fast for me. This is. Should the tour man. This before I. Should scared.

Incredibly disorientated, Grey opened his eyes. He was on Wiggle Island and had passed out momentarily. His vision was blurred, for there was something stuck in his eyelid. Further inspection of this thing induced a great sharp pain, so Grey left it alone - he really hated pain. The ride had now stopped and the bars had been raised, but it took Grey a small large while to gather himself before disembarking. As he walked across the soft orange clay floor, his legs were jelly-like causing him to stumble.

The sky was black, yet the island was strangely illuminated somehow. It was completely made up of this orange clay that stuck to Grey's shoes as he walked. A blue, square headed Wiggle came up to Grey and walked alongside him. Grey noticed its eyes. He had forgotten about Wiggle eyes. Grey looked down and smiled at the Wiggle - it smiled back.

'Staying here long hey?' It asked, in a squeaky tone.

'As long as I can...'

'You sound really weary and what's that in your eye hey?'

'I don't know it's...'

'Shall I have a look at it? Wiggles like me are very clever at all sorts of problems...'

'No thank you, it's very painful, not that I'm afraid of pain, but I'd prefer a Normal doctor to look at it,'

'Okie-doke hey'

The Wiggle then continued to walk next to Grey as he approached the stone bridge that crossed the green swamps and would eventually lead him to the main factory gate.

Feeling slightly peckish, Grey picked up the Wiggle by its neck and bit off the lower half of its torso and legs.

'Bye!' it called, although its mouth was filled now with dark blue Wiggle-blood reducing its attempts to talk to more of a gurgle.

'Oh, sorry I forgot, bye-bye Wiggly!' Grey said, before finishing off his snack and licking his fingers. Pure fresh Wiggle is so much better than that pre-packed stuff they sell in the supermarkets.

Grey approached the Gate. Wiggles were hurriedly buzzing about the entrance, totally oblivious to Grey - they were getting on with their midday tasks - excavating Toilifu and transporting it into small openings that scattered the factory walls, planting crops into the orange clay and setting challenges for the Normals in the toll booths that stretched out along the riverbank for as far as Grey could see. He had only been here twice before, and it always surprised him how hectic it was considering how peaceful Wiggles are usually.

Grey stood much taller than all of the Wiggles and so when continuing toward the gate, he found it difficult not to crush a few. The intercom was operated by other Normals who live permanently on Wiggle-Island. He pressed the button.

'Hi this is Grey Foster, I've booked a room in suite thirty-two.'

'Come right in.' Replied a female receptionist. She sounded a bit like Lynn, to be fair. Although Grey had sworn that he wasn't to think about her for his stay here, he found it hard to block her out of his mind completely. The door latch opened and Grey began to make his way toward the large map mounted in the centre of the hallway. The interior was all painted a very clean and smooth peachy tone; the floor made up of pure white plastic and the ceiling was arched. The place reminded Grey of an airport, with all its signs, shops and escalators. Inside the factory foyer there were ironically more Normals than Wiggles, and when Grey began to study the map, a couple of porter-Wiggles surrounded him, ready to take his bag.

'Room thirty-two please,' Grey said, 'and please could you wait up there for when I get back, I'm still a bit peckish.'

'Sure thing chappie!'

After the Wiggles had scurried off, he studied the map carefully. As he read the map, searching for the hospital so that he could treat his eye, his hands began to slowly twist and contort out of shape.

'Oh how could I forget about *this* palaver!' Smiled Grey.

It is a common side-effect of a Normal existing in the underground factories that their hands buckle under the strain after touching any Wiggle (the condition is known as 'Wiggle-hand' or 'Greed-fingering' Fig.1 p76). It is not a serious ailment, since the hands return to their original form upon the travellers' arrival home, but the 'horrific' deformity appals so many people who visit, that they never do return. To many, the very thought of it is so distressing that they don't ever visit - this alone constitutes as the largest factor limiting Slap Tourism in the Wiggle factories. Special gloves are available to prevent Wiggle-hand altogether yet these have never been largely popular due to high costs.

Whilst Grey *was* really on holiday, he also had a hidden business agenda - over the past few decades, Wiggles have become renowned as high-quality Novelty Wood (fig.2 p77) manufacturers and Grey was hoping to take back a large stock for resale. Technically this practice is illegal, since only official companies are permitted to bring back Novelty Wood as a measure of regulation to prevent the supply becoming saturated. Yet, Grey had friends in high places and what's more - a review of Ben Wheele's Novelty Wood was recently undertaken (see p75) of which only Grey and a few others were aware. This was likely to further boost - or even *rocket* their sales when he returned home.

Under normal circumstances he wouldn't attempt to smuggle any Novelty Wood due to the high risks involved (if Wiggles become angry it's not unheard of for them to set a 'bad' challenge - whereby, for example, this guy was once tricked into killing his own daughter and then completely forgetting what had happened) but this really was a special case - Grey silently imagined how many Ezlo notes he would receive back home and began to cry.